GROUP
COUNSELING

SUCCESSFUL PASTORAL COUNSELING SERIES

GROUP COUNSELING

JOSEPH W. KNOWLES

PRENTICE-HALL, INC., ENGLEWOOD CLIFFS, N.J.

Group Counseling
by Joseph W. Knowles

© 1964 by Prentice-Hall, Inc.,
Englewood Cliffs, New Jersey

Library of Congress Catalog Card Number: 64–12849

Printed in the United States of America.   T   36537

PRENTICE-HALL INTERNATIONAL, INC., *London*
PRENTICE-HALL OF AUSTRALIA, PTY., LTD., *Sydney*
PRENTICE-HALL OF CANADA, LTD., *Toronto*
PRENTICE-HALL FRANCE, S.A.R.L., *Paris*
PRENTICE-HALL OF INDIA (PRIVATE) LTD., *New Delhi*
PRENTICE-HALL OF JAPAN, INC., *Tokyo*
PRENTICE-HALL DE MEXICO, S.A., *Mexico City*

*To Betty and Kathy,
my wife and daughter
from whom I have learned
most concerning the nature
and meaningfulness of being
in community*

INTRODUCTION

This series of books represents the most comprehensive publishing effort ever made in the field of pastoral care. These books could not have been published twenty-five years ago or probably even ten, for the material was not then available. In the past, single books have been available covering different phases of the task. Now we are bringing the subjects together in a single series. Here we present a library of pastoral care covering the major topics and problems that most pastors will encounter in their ministry. Fortunately, not all of these problems need be faced every week or even every month. But, when they are, the minister wants help and he wants it immediately.

These books are prepared for the nonspecialized minister serving the local church, where he is the most accessible professional person in the community. It is a well-accepted fact that more people turn to clergy when in trouble than to all other professional people. Therefore, the pastor must not fail them.

Russell L. Dicks
General Editor

PREFACE

This book is an offspring of courtship and conflict, engagement and marriage of the author's clinical and theological perspectives. For five years as chaplain supervisor in a state psychiatric hospital in Kentucky, he searched for a clinical and theological understanding of personality and means of ministry to distressed individuals. As a director of a pastoral counseling center engaging primarily in family counseling in Los Angeles for four years, he and the staff came to appreciate the interlocking, complementary nature of family relationships and their spiritual significance.

Focus upon group counseling and doctrines of church and ministry were natural next steps while teaching in a clinical pastoral education program at the Institute of Religion, Texas Medical Center, Houston, Texas. This progression from *individual* to *family* to *group counseling* has led to a current exploration of the *church as a reconciling community* and of the healing potential within its interrelated, small subgroups.

This clinical and theological pilgrimage has therefore moved from microcosm toward macrocosm—from an attempt at understanding the individual and pastoral counseling with individuals to understanding the interrelationships between the person and his significant groups and the ministry of pastoral group counseling. Like most marriages and their offspring, there is yet much room for correction and growth. Hopefully, the path has an open end.

The book is based upon the thesis that group counseling is integral to the ministry of the church. The doctrines of church and ministry reveal the depth nature of a counseling group, and a counseling group can become a means of grace whereby the church is enabled to *be* the church. Furthermore, the ministry of the church is the ministry of the entire people of God. Group counseling can become

PREFACE

one means by which the pastor fulfills his essential function "to equip God's people for work in his service" (Ephesians 4:11–12 NEB) and through which laymen perform their priesthood as members of the Body of Christ.

The author is indebted to many people for their instructive, shaping influences. Only a few can be named: Wayne E. Oates, Th.D., Southern Baptist Theological Seminary; David Eitzen, Ph.D., Southern California School of Theology, Claremont, California; Aaron Rutledge, Th.D., Merril-Palmer School, Detroit, Michigan; Charles Yoke, M.D., psychiatrist, Hot Springs, Arkansas; David Mendel, M.D., and Eugene Tips, M.D., group psychotherapists in Houston, Texas. The reader will note frequent references to the work of George R. Bach, Ph.D., a clinical psychologist in Los Angeles, California.

The Reverend Russell Dicks has made pertinent suggestions as well as offering the initial invitation to write in this series, of which he is editor.

Members of the Church of the Saviour, Washington, D.C., gave time for writing and their enthusiastic support. Specific members have participated in the book's preparation: Miss Kathryn Campbell edited the first draft and made many helpful suggestions. Mrs. Thelma Hemker and Mrs. Paul Miller contributed their secretarial services.

Members of counseling groups in Houston, Texas, and in Washington, D.C., have been major contributors through their participation in the counseling process and permitting an appropriation of group events to make this writing more concrete. All names used are fictitious.

Joseph W. Knowles

CONTENTS

CONTENTS

Part I

GROUP COUNSELING IN THE CONTEXT

OF THE CHURCH AND ITS MINISTRY

CHAPTER ONE

The NATURE Of GROUP COUNSELING

Group counseling may be a new approach to ministry for the pastor but the idea that healing occurs in communion and community is not new. The church's historic witness is that redemption and healing occur as persons are reunited in fellowship with God and with His people. Group counseling embodies a philosophy of healing as well as a methodolgy. It takes into account the communal aspects of man's nature and the healing potential within experiences of community. This understanding of human personality is essential to an understanding of how healing takes place in small groups.

Personality Theory and
Group Counseling Methodology

The practice of counseling and psychotherapy in the past decade has enlarged its views of man. Sigmund Freud based his work on a biological, deterministic understanding of human nature. Now, psychotherapists have corrected Freud's point of view; the discoveries of sociology and anthropology could not be ignored. The biological organism is not the only *given* in the development of personality. A person does not become a human being except in the context of community. It is the community of the family, the neighborhood, the church, that calls forth the individual. The family gives the child a position, affirms him, and takes account of him. The family calls him to assume responsibilities appropriate to his level or degree of maturity. It gives him his earliest values and meanings and grants him the means and context wherein to find satisfactions of biological needs and security for emotional growth and interpersonal adventure. In other words, one discovers his identity and fulfills his potential in experiences of community. This involves becoming a participant member who influences others and who responds in turn to their acts.

This changing view of man has opened up new methods of counseling and psychotherapy. The term "pastoral counseling" often refers to counseling with one individual or with married couples. Best results are gained when counseling is with more than one of the members involved in a problem situation. When the counseling pastor reaches out to include more than the "problem person," he overtly or intuitively is aware of the interlocking nature of human relationships. It is difficult for a person to change unless change also takes place in others who are interwoven into the mesh of one's interpersonal relationships. Each takes a role or a mode of relating and communicating, which is either complementary or conflictual to the interpersonal behavior of the other. Change in one calls for modification in the other, in order to preserve balance and complementarity.

Society is not only outside the individual but also inside him. The self emerges as one becomes aware of biological and instinctual needs within oneself and identifies these as belonging to one's own personality; but one's selfhood also includes social experience growing out of interaction with other individuals. Furthermore, the developing person absorbs within himself the feelings, attitudes, and values of other persons significant to him; such internalization provides the ground for understanding, relating to, and communicating with others. (Freud used the word "identification" for this process, but this term does not fully express how the process equips one for social participation.)

Members of a family or church at times relate, and are related to, in such a way as to call forth unloving and alienating responses from each other. At this point, they need counseling in order to discover the nature of their personal and relational brokenness and to discover "a more perfect way" of seeing and hearing and communicating and responding. Group counseling is a most fertile situation in which individuals gain personal insight and find power to effect personal change.

Group counseling takes into account the interlocking nature of interpersonal relationships and the way in which the address of one calls for a reciprocal response in the other. When such address and response become an unhealthy pattern or one that spells conflict, the person is trapped. For example, a group member tells how her mother manipulates and controls her. Her response to the mother, both as a child and an adult, becomes habitual compliance to the demands of the mother or to any other person to whom she is related in an emotionally significant way. This pattern has developed in the social context of the small group—the family. Furthermore, the pattern persists in other interpersonal relationships.

Group counseling as a methodology lays hold upon the reality situation in which life began, develops, and continues—the social reality of relatedness in small groups. In the family and other significant social situations, unsuccessful patterns of relating have been learned. The group method seizes upon this understanding and is based on the expectancy that, in a situation similar to that of the family, a matrix is available for re-education and for correction of unhealthy and conflictual styles of relating.

An understanding of the nature of group counseling commends it as a meaningful method of ministry to the pastor. Its quantitative and qualitative distinctives and values make it a "medicine of choice." An exploration of the nature of group counseling reveals unique therapeutic resources not inherent in individual counseling.

Quantitative Values of Group Counseling

A primary reason for the group approach to counseling is that it enables the church to serve more persons in less time or to serve a few over a longer duration of time.

Need for Counseling Resources. Recent surveys reveal that 87 per cent of city dwellers acknowledge struggles with personal and family problems and that 42 per cent turn first to the pastor and the church. The ministry of counseling makes heavy inroads on the pastor's time, which must be apportioned to other functions of his ministry also. Group counseling opens a way for the professional or lay minister to serve six to nine people in the same amount of time that could otherwise be devoted to only one person. The minister who spends six hours a week counseling six individuals can counsel 24 to 36 in the same amount of time. Extra time would be required to screen and prepare members for a group, but once groups were established, this would be minimal.

Duration of Counseling Extended. Not only can a greater number of people be cared for, but each can be given more time if he belongs to a group. Few pastors can afford to spend several hours with one individual, and in many cases the counseling has to end with only one or two visits. For a very few, intensive counseling may continue for 6 to 12 interviews.

But a pastor can give intensive attention to a small group. To translate this into group counseling statistics: the six persons receiving a total of six hours each would have twenty-four hours of counseling instead of six hours, and in the same amount of time the pastor extends his relationship from six weeks to six months with each person. This method will appeal to pastoral counselors who fulfill their ministry best in a long-term relationship.

Qualitative Values of Group Counseling

Earl D. Marsh points toward the uniqueness of the method in his well-known words, "By the crowd they have been broken; by the crowd they shall be healed." It would be more specific to say, "By the group they have been broken and by the group they shall be healed." The way that others, who are significant to us in groups of which we are a member, feel about us and relate to us shapes the *perceptual image* of ourself, of others, and even of God. These "significant others," to use Mead's[1] term, also determine how *we feel* about ourselves and how *we act* toward others and to God. This is especially true during our formative years.

A therapeutic group provides a new family or peer group in which each member can have corrective experiences. This is possible for several reasons.

A Problem-Solving Family or Peer Group. In the first place, an individual tends to restructure his original family in each new significant group he belongs to. In a counseling group, he finds persons like himself and members who are like his father, his mother, siblings, and others—grandparents, uncles, aunts. The married person can identify feelings and patterns of behavior in other group members that are similar to those of significant people in his own contemporary family, church, social, and occupational groups.

Herein lies the genius of group counseling. One is given a complex of relationships in which members act out their problems in relation to each other. They experience, help each other to become

[1] George Herbert Mead, *Mind, Self and Society* (Chicago: University of Chicago Press, 1934).

aware of, and together seek to alter patterns of behavior that are defeating them and others. In the social situation of the group, these self-defeating patterns are objectified so that all may see, accept, and labor together toward more constructive modes of communicating and relating.

To illustrate:

Tony: Barbara and I have two close friends with whom we get together often. We sit around talking, and somehow the conversation gets around in a semi-joking way—but underneath the joking you know that there is fire under the smoke—about my deficiencies as a husband. I have a lot of hobbies I enjoy, like puttering in the workshop or tinkering with the car. She says I don't like to dance any more as I did before we were married, or I don't like to play tennis any more. These little things to me seem to be such superficial and minor deficiencies in marriage because basically in our relationship real camaraderie is there but apparently (Laughs) my wife doesn't share my conviction about this at times. At times she gets in moods where she feels we really don't have much in common. I think we have a tremendous amount in common. She cites other couples who do things together. It seems that she complains I am not made in her image, but I don't always like things she likes to do . . . this happens periodically. I don't know whether this is something that is true or whether it is a projection of her feelings or a mood. It seems this is something about which I do not know what to do. I can change my actions but not my interest.

Tony went on to say that his wife grew up without brothers from whom she could learn to appreciate masculine interests. On the other hand, he grew up in a family of all boys. Perhaps, he mused, there was something basically different between male and female. Some of the problems growing out of sex differences seem insoluble to him.

His wife notices that he really enjoys seeing special friends come over for a visit. "You let yourself go and seem to have such a good time together." Also, he has observed, she reacts negatively to other people's compliments to her about him.

Counselor: Let me ask a question. Is there something Barbara feels that she is missing out on in the relationship?

Tony: Are you asking me?

Counselor: Either you or the group.

Tony: I think she misses sharing my absorption in my daily work. From 9 to 5 I am living in another world which she cannot share.

Julie: You work with things at home and with people in the daytime?

Tony: This is new and interesting. Could you elaborate further?

Julie: You are very outgoing with other people, kind and considerate of them, but as you describe the relationship at home, you seem to withdraw. You don't have the same outgoing relationship with Barbara as you have with other people. You are a good mixer as I know you.

Tony: (Coughs)

Julie: (Continuing) The fact is, if I were in Barbara's place, I would be very jealous.

Counselor: Hmmm! You'd be very jealous!

Julie: Yes!

Tony: What? Of the things I'm interested in?

Julie: No, of the fact that you are this way with people and a different way with me.

In the ensuing discussion, Tony noted that Barbara's father always went out of his way to help people outside the family but would never "turn his hand" to help a member of his own family. He commented, "This could tie in with what you are saying. If I have lots of attention to give to everyone else, Barbara feels I don't have any to give to her." Later in the discussion, Julie focused on her own marital relationship. She commented that this discussion was helpful because it threw light on her relationship with her husband. She saw much similarity between Tony and her husband in their ability to be outgoing, pleasing, friendly, and nice to people outside the family but having the tendency to withdraw in their own home. Ralph, a third member of the group who had been relatively nonparticipative, moved in and appropriated the discussion, noting that his job, part of which he did at home, occupied his time when his wife wanted to talk with him. By the time he finished his job and was ready to talk, his wife was exasperated to the point of anger.

The above excerpt concretely demonstrates a core dimension of group counseling. Julie literally identifies with Tony's wife; Julie is able to say to him what Barbara could not. Julie tells Tony that if she were his wife she would be very jealous because of the emotional gift of himself to other people and the neglect of his wife. Julie can identify with Tony's wife because she herself feels neglected by her own husband. Ralph appropriates the encounter between Tony and Julie and begins to explore one of the sources of turbulence in his relationship with his wife. Although the group spotlight focused upon Tony for a major portion of the session, two other members of the group were at the same time dealing with their own marital problems.

The Group's Unique Structure and Gifts. These corrective events, in the second place, can occur because the counseling group is different from other social groups. It is not just another class meeting but has a unique climate, covenant, and purpose that distinguish it from other social situations.

The *emotional climate of a therapeutic group* affords the freedom, with others, to be what one is, to feel what one feels, and to communicate what one really feels and thinks. Healing and redemption can take place. In most social situations, including the church, unfortunately, very definite lines are drawn as to what behavior is permissible. A person stays within these boundaries or he is not accepted.

The climate of acceptance and freedom allows each member to drop his guardedness and censoring of what he feels and thinks. The oversocialized person especially learns that the best gift he has to offer the group is his immediate, spontaneous, uncensored experience. The counselor and the group cultivate this climate. Individual counseling grants similar gifts but only in relationship to one other person, the counselor.

This climate does not at first exist; the group, with the assistance of the counselor, has to cultivate it and overcome the underlying fear of being criticized, exposed, and disapproved of by the other members. Each person first needs to put his best foot or face forward by revealing only strengths and adequacies. Each needs the approval of others, as well as self-approval. Before group members get down to where it hurts, they test out the group, much as a timid bather first dips his toe in a pool. Freedom to be spontaneous comes only as members come to trust each other.

We now see the *covenant nature of the group*. Members make a formal covenant to keep the confidences; what comes out in the sessions is the "property of the group." They may talk freely with each other but not with nongroup members. This kind of commitment facilitates trustful communication. Real trust comes when each is assured that he will be heard, that he is respected, that he is included as a valued member and that the group cares for him as a person in his own right. With this bond of trust, members can afford to reveal the "good me" and the "bad me." Herein lies the difference from most other social groups, except perhaps the family.

The purpose or goal of the counseling group is a third reason why it is different from other classes or meetings in the church. Any effective group must be clear as to its reason for being—its task. That of a therapeutic group is the healing of the conflict and guilt within the person and the brokenness and alienation in his relationships with others, including God. The climate and the covenant of trust described above make it possible to be what one is within the group. An individual begins to assimilate and integrate into himself that part of himself which he has previously hidden from the view of all, and often from himself. This represents change and movement, the dropping of the mask, and becoming more real and authentic.

Healing requires changes of modes of relating and communicating. Can I love and accept others as they are? Can I hear what others are saying and respond to their needs, strivings, and values? Each begins to see, through the other members' eyes, how he is experienced by others. These people who allow him to become who he is also help him to evaluate what his behavior does to others. Here we encounter the *paradox of acceptance and judgment in redemptive counseling*.

George Bach[2] points out that the group adheres to the principle that everything anybody does, says, or thinks, which involves another member of the group, is subject to open discussion by the group. What one does to others in relationships is most clearly focused in the critical encounters between members. Members may interact in such a way as to let each other know when they are hurt or helped, when they feel loved or hated by another member. Such encounters are often very difficult in other social groups, but in the therapeutic group, protection is built in. The counselor provides this protection as he helps the group objectify and reflect on what happens. The group itself provides protection: members will come to the defense of one unjustly treated or too threatened by a confrontation.

In this paradox of acceptance and judgment, each element contributes toward healing. The confrontation enables the person to see clearly, and the acceptance, support, and love provide him with strength and courage to evaluate himself and to modify unconstructive patterns of behavior.

The *size of the group* contributes a fourth unique structural element. If there are fewer than five in the group, a member is able to control both his own action and communication and to control the group, and this will prevent his difficulties from coming to light. For example:

Sarah: [in a group of seven] I find it difficult to share with you. There seem to be just too many of you. If there were only two or three, I would find it easier to talk. But with this many people, I just don't know how you are going to react.

Counselor: Sarah, you would feel more comfortable, sure of yourself and others, if we were a smaller group?

Sarah: Yes, I would.

Counselor: I wonder if you are telling us that you find it difficult to trust yourself to seven people instead of three? Are you able to edit and screen what you say [in a smaller group] and make sure what you share is acceptable?

[2] See *Intensive Group Psychotherapy* (New York: The Ronald Press, 1954), p. 30.

Sarah: (Her eyes widening) How interesting! I always needed the approval of other people. I suppose I'm afraid I will not be accepted in this group.

When the group is too small, there is too little possibility for multiple interactional relationship. A person suffers the same sort of limitations in a group of three or four that the child faces in a family of equal size. The opportunity for developing "object relationships" and multiple "role relationships" is enhanced in a larger family or group. A child with two parents and three or four siblings has obvious advantages over the only child, or two children with only one parent. When only two or three members show up for a meeting, there will be a tendency toward counseling one member.

Other problems appear when the group is too large. Time in each session is insufficient for each to get involved in depth. Parishioners become frustrated if several come to the group with pressing concerns and are blocked by others equally suffering. In addition, less aggressive members face greater difficulty in participating in a large group. The writer believes that optimum size is seven or eight members.

The *time factor* poses a fifth element of structure. Individual counseling has glorified the 50-minute hour, although this image is in process of being broken. Group counseling requires a minimum of 90 minutes to allow group involvement to develop and time for each member's use. A few counselors consider a two-hour period preferable, but an hour-and-a-half period will suffice.

Another aspect of the time element is the duration of life of a group, which may be an "open" or an "end" group. The *open group* is one which continues. When a member feels he has derived maximum benefit, he announces his intention to leave the group. He tests the decision with the group and leaves if he feels his decision is a wise one. The counselor then fills the vacancy with a new member. The *end group* has a terminal date for all members. They know they have three, six, or nine months in which to be together. Best results are obtained with a six- to nine-month group.

Well-motivated members appropriate the benefits of a group for a period of one year or longer. The pastor's interest and the time available will determine his time commitment to a group. Pastors can contribute to this field by experimenting with different durations of time scheduled for a group and sharing their observations of what can be accomplished in varying time spans. In Chapter 4, short-term groups are discussed.

Unique Advantages in Leadership. Further unique advantages of group counseling are seen from a perspective of leadership. In individual counseling, the pastor is the only counselor in the situation. In a group, there are as many counselors as there are members, plus the leader. Each member at points becomes the counselor for another member. Group members listen, accept, support, clarify, confront, and interpret. These are counselor functions.

This shared responsibility means that the members come to depend primarily on each other for help. On the whole, group members direct their remarks to each other, not to the leader. They *look* to each other for the resolution of their difficulty. The *dependency relationship* that is often formed with the pastor in individual counseling is thus transferred from the pastor to the group. This is the same dynamic at work as that which operates in adolescence. Dependency is shifted from parents to the peer group, and a move toward autonomy is strengthened—precursor of a move toward interdependence in group relationships.

Furthermore, other transference reactions toward the counselor are attenuated. Members tend to express their hostile, angry, ambivalent, jealous, hurt, loving, and appreciative feelings toward one another. Interpretations that members make for one another are not weighted with the same kind of authority that they would be coming from the pastor. He has an authority role in which members invest him with power and wisdom, and his insight cannot be lightly accepted or dismissed. The following comment comes from a group member:

"Richard, you are one of us. Thomas [the counselor] may have his weaknesses and problems but I don't know what they are. But I know you. You are in the same kind of mess that all of the rest of us are in." Because of this awareness, a member can more easily accept what another member says to him. He can also more easily deny, reject, or do battle with his peer.

This does not mean that the counselor will not come in for his share of testing. He will. He is an authority person in the group and authority problems of members will be evident in their relationship to him. He is not, however, the only representative of authority present. A member may represent an authority figure to another member simply because he reminds him of such a person, either past or contemporary.

To a certain extent, each member is an authority and also gets his share of transference reactions from his peers. To illustrate, this happened when a new member came into a group. An older member had previously exercised a leadership role in the group. Later in the meeting he turned to the new member and said, "I think I ought to tell you I am very angry with you. You have come in and taken over the place I have had in the group. In fact, you are sitting in *my* chair."

Lastly, the pastor finds a way to help the noncommunicative type of parishioner. Some people have difficulty verbalizing. Pastors know the difficulty of counseling with silent counselees. In a group, the nonverbal person finds help through what Raymond J. Corsini calls "spectator therapy."[3] Often a person may just sit and observe. This does not mean he is not involved with what is going on; he may be deeply involved—in fact, so much so that he does not feel safe at the moment to reveal what is going on within him. Members will permit a person to participate this way. They respect the difficulty in becoming verbally participative. They defend the right of a person to wait until he is secure enough and free enough to share.

The group will not ignore the silent member, however. Members have a way of picking up his nonverbal communications, such as, "I notice that Mark seemed to agree with Katherine. Mark nodded his head vigorously and clenched his fist." Eventually, the group will focus on the silent member if he remains so for several sessions. One will say, for example, "Mark, I have had the feeling that you are with us but you have not spoken very much. I really don't know you, but I would like to know you." Herein is both invitation and expectation to open one's self to the group and to claim one's birthright of membership in the healing community.

[3] *Methods of Group Psychotherapy* (New York: McGraw-Hill Book Co., Inc., 1957).

CHAPTER TWO

The CONTEXT Of GROUP COUNSELING

As a passage of Scripture cannot be grasped out of context, so does a discussion of group counseling need to be put in the context of its setting. When the church is the setting, it shapes and enriches this method of ministry. An understanding of the nature of the church thus contributes to an understanding of the process. There are two aspects of the effect of the church context on group counseling.

Operational Meanings. The person counseled will bring certain meanings to the process he experiences with a church group, and the pastoral counselor needs to be aware of these meanings and how they affect the counseling relationship. He should also be aware of elements of the structure which he, as pastor, brings to the relationship.

Seward Hiltner and Lowell G. Colston identify four contextual elements[1] in counseling in the church:

1. Setting, or the physical plant, with its symbols and symbolic meanings.
2. Expectations of the client.
3. Shifts in relationship in which the pastor is not only counselor but is related in other social roles, such as preacher, teacher, and guest in one's home.
4. The limits of the pastor as a counselor and the limits of the goals of his counseling.

These four elements have positive and/or negative valence for the ideas and feelings of persons in counseling. A church setting presents problems for some. One man said to the writer, "I don't want counseling from an agency that has the word 'pastoral' con-

[1] *The Context of Pastoral Counseling* (New York: Abingdon Press, 1961), pp. 29–31.

nected with its name." Others are like the woman who confided, "I feel safe and secure with you in the counseling room, but when I meet you outside I am afraid of you. I wonder what you must think of me after all I have told you." Thus is the pastor limited by his popular image, which may be that of one who is completely above or out of touch with earthly desires and problems, or of one who is bound to sit in judgment.

Occasionally, a church member will resist referral to a psychotherapist and press the pastor to accept counseling responsibility which, ethically, he cannot assume. Some feel more secure with a known and trusted person; sometimes they fear the loss of unhealthy religious defenses that might have to be dropped or be ruthlessly dealt with by a secular psychiatrist. They are unaware that most psychotherapists will not make an assault upon the security system of a person but will instead create the kind of situation where defenses are no longer necessary. The defenses may then be explored in safety and eventually discarded for more fruitful forms of goal-seeking.

On the other hand, the writer concurs with the positive findings of Hiltner and Colston, who discover evidence for their hypothesis that "people seeking counseling help from a pastor, when other conditions are approximately equal, will tend to progress slightly farther and faster in the same amount of time than they will in another setting. . . ."[2] In a church where members engage in depth dialogue with each other, the word "slightly" can be changed to "significantly." Five of the seven counseling groups at the Church of the Saviour in Washington, D.C., moved to a level in one month that would have taken six months for groups in a nonchurch setting to achieve. Such rapid progress was due to movement in relationship that preceded and accompanied involvement in a counseling group. The other two groups needed three months (still only half the usual time) to get past their resistance in order to become "a working group."

Theological Perspective. A second element that contributes to the context is the theological perspective, especially the counselor's view of the church and its ministry. Franklin Segler says: "A theology of the church and its ministry is basic to a theology of the pastoral ministry. The nature of the church determines the nature

[2] *Ibid.*, p. 21.

of the pastor's task. Indeed, the church's ministry is the pastor's ministry."[3]

The pastor brings to his counseling work a concept of God and a theology of man, the world, the nature of the church and its ministry. He also makes use of specific spiritual resources such as prayer, Scripture, and sacraments. In others words, he is a *pastoral* counselor because of his role as shepherd of the congregation, his theological perspective, and his spiritual resources.

Group counseling has emerged in fields and contexts outside the church, and the pastor does well to inquire if this new wineskin is integral to the nature of the church and its ministry. How does it become a means of grace? Without such assurance he may experience division within and wonder if he has imported a method alien to the community of faith. Likewise, the person counseled is helped to accept the method if he can understand it as a process through which he may clarify and deepen his commitment to Christ and grow up within His Body.

Group Counseling and the Nature of the Church

The doctrine of the church provides the model for group counseling; such a process thus becomes a means by which the nature and being of the church are actualized. The church as a body of the forgiven should be able to mediate love and healing in a purposeful way.

The Church As Event. In a day in which the church has become too completely identified with its institutional life and structures, we need to experience a renewal of the idea that the church is Event. It is primarily the act of God calling into being a people to worship and serve Him. Claude Welch[4] reminds us that the church is *congregatio,* a congregation, because of God's *convocatio,* His call. God acts through Jesus Christ to call unto Himself a people. The church exists as an act of God who loves the world and its inhabitants and who calls His people unto Himself.

The church's being, however, depends not only on the acts of

[3] *A Theology of Church and Ministry* (Nashville: Broadman Press, 1960), p. 3.
[4] *The Reality of the Church* (New York: Charles Scribner's Sons, 1958), p. 64 ff.

God in the past. Any church that is alive is so because God is its Life, acting within it in the present. The Holy Spirit is more than a doctrine; He is God in Christ alive, active, and at work in His world and in His church in the world. God is not dead to those who acknowledge His sovereignty and who seek to live in obedience before Him as His servant in the world.

Each pastor is well aware of the tendency of the church to identify itself with its outward forms which have not the presence and power of God in them. Often our preaching witnesses to what God has done in the past but neglects what He does in the present. Doctrinal preaching and teaching of the Word are often divorced from the deed and truth. The Event of Jesus Christ also is the Word that God continues to be at work through the ministry of the Holy Spirit to complete the conquest of evil and to deliver His people from bondage.

In a counseling group, relational events occur. At times, the group members advise and intellectualize with one another, but more significant are the moments of encounter. These face-to-face events at times become Events—the moments of God's acts to forgive, reconcile, and heal in the context of this small community.

A member announced that the pastor's wife, a person significant to each group member, was faced with major surgery. The group was stunned, because Marjorie had never been seriously ill before. Group members wished to begin the session with prayer. This led to the following encounter:

Counselor: Are you saying we need to spend a part of our time now in prayer for Marjorie and her family?

Amos: Could we talk about this a little bit more? I can't really pray about it until I get my own feelings better clarified. (Silence) Because the thing I feel so sharply at a time like this is the question of death . . . and also another thing is the impact on the family of the church.

Amelia: Why do we think about death at this point? Why do we leap into this? (Laughs nervously and apologizes) I'm sorry I interrupted.

Amos: No, that's all right. Why do you feel that this is not the right response, the appropriate response? To make it more critical, why don't you have this response?

Amelia: Well, I have the immediate response that we ought to triumphantly offer Marjorie to God without any thought about what this [the surgery] may mean.

Elizabeth: How do you do this, Amelia? When we prayed for Amy Ballentine, most of us prayed at first for ourselves in order to get our own feeling out of the way. . . . We were aware we needed to offer her, but our feelings kept getting in the way. . . . And my immediate feeling was one of fear in relation to Marjorie.

Amos: It's really a fear about death, then?

Elizabeth: Well, when you push it back, it really is. And she represents the family as far as I am concerned. And I think she does in a sense to all of us. I'm not saying that . . . this is wonderful, Amelia, but I can't do it.

Cecil: Is what you are saying, "Almost our first concern is what's going to happen to us, what's going to happen to Paul, what's going to happen to the church?" In other words, we turn it in. Is that right?

Amos: My first reaction was anxiety and fear over Marjorie's death.

Cecil: No, I don't mean that . . .

Amelia: I don't feel that it's so. (With great feeling) If you all want to talk about this you just call me when you are through. (Gets up and walks out of the room)

Other group members joined in. Several felt that it was an automatic reaction that one would think about the possibility of death and this had to be faced before the matter could be relinquished. John, who had not spoken previously, sought to interpret Amelia's remarks. He felt Amelia was saying, "We ought to pray for Marjorie's deepest healing." He went on to explain that such healing had nothing to do with physical healing and could mean death. The person may be dying and death is not to be feared if this is the deepest healing. He added, "I think I would have put it differently. I think my immediate reaction is, 'What on earth are you telling us here, God?' Here is where my feelings get in the way. Things have meaning, dramatic meaning." The group responded as follows:

Counselor:	My first reaction was the possibility of death and my prayer when I first heard the news took this into account.
Amos:	(Exploding) Why did you not say that when Amelia was here? I would rather she walked out because of your saying this than me. (Group laughs loudly)
Counselor:	Others in the group voiced the same reaction. I wonder why Amos feels responsible for Amelia's leaving.
Amos:	I feel upset because Amelia has rejected me and my feelings about death.
Corinne:	She hasn't rejected you . . .
Amos:	(Interrupting) She has! No matter what she did and how the group interprets what she did, she has not helped me in my moment of need to deal with death and anxiety and anxiety about death. So she has left me then . . . and I had a real feeling of support from Amelia. So if Amelia had not been someone who supported me, it would not have mattered that she left. When Amelia leaves the room, she leaves me with nothing but fear and anxiety and her support is gone, so here I sit now.

The group moved in to minister to Amos. At one point, Corinne expressed concern for Amelia, saying, "I think she is having the worst of this thing. We have each other, but Amelia is out there alone." The group talked on. Finally Corinne arose, saying, "I feel I ought to go out to be with Amelia." The group assented and she left. In a few minutes, Amelia and Corinne re-entered the room. While outside, Corinne had explained her concern for Amelia and Amos's feeling of rejection by Amelia. As soon as she entered, Amelia went over to Amos, embraced him, and quietly said, "Forgive me, Amos. I suppose I was feeling more deeply for Marjorie than about you."

This excerpt demonstrates the nature of the counseling group in the church setting as Event. Here the reality of sickness, death, the need for God's assistance, and appropriation of the resource of prayer are experienced as well as discussed. Looking upon the event within the group from the eyes of faith, we can see God at work through the group. Here He cares for a member of the fellowship who is

ill. We can see God at work through group members to help one
another face the fear and anxiety of death and to begin to accept
this reality with lessened threat. The most significant event was the
reconciling work of Christ through the Holy Spirit who prompts one
member to care for two estranged persons. This member becomes
an agent of God's reconciliation. The person "outside the door" re-
turns, makes confession, and is reunited with her community. She
is also reunited at a deeper level with the one member who needed
her most.

The Church as the Covenant Community. The church and
the counseling group have in common the covenant nature of their
fellowship. The God revealed in the history of the nation, Israel,
and in the history of the Christian Community is the God of the
Covenant. As a covenant-making God, He binds himself in love to
His people. He is faithful and does not leave or forsake them. They
may rebel and defy him, but He is faithful. At times His love is
experienced as corrective discipline, but the God of the Old and the
New Covenant continues to stand in relationship to those whom He
has chosen.

Because God is faithful, the people of God are in covenant not
only to be faithful to Him but to be committed in love to one another. In fact, their commitment to one another is grounded in and
a witness to God's faithfulness to His own. The problem arises
because God's people are covenant-breakers. They fall away from
faithful commitment to each other. The world of impersonality,
hostility, envy, search for power and glory invades the church. It
becomes the community where relationships are superficial and
distant. People do not stand with, meet, and become involved in
depth with one another.

The counseling group in the context of the church takes the
covenant to one another seriously. Members covenant to hold in
confidence that which is shared in the context of the group. Each
learns that he can share himself fully without being gossiped about.
He finds a community that is faithful to honor the trust that he invests in it.

The covenant operates at an even deeper level. Each member finds
that a group will stay with him *in spite of* who he is and what he
does in the group. In most social groups, even in the church, each
person screens his behavior carefully. To be accepted, a person feels

he must be acceptable. But the counseling group is faithful to hear and to respond to each member, to face and meet each other. When a member violates the covenant, the group disciplines him. Nor does the group ignore the unobtrusive member. Patiently, it will wait for the person to "say something." Eventually, the group will turn and make overtures to include the silent observer and to take him into the fellowship.

The counseling group, therefore, helps church members learn what it means to belong to a covenant community. In such a group, the idea of the church as a covenant people becomes concrete in the history of the experiences of group members. Within such experiences, the word of God's faithfulness takes on vital meaning. The counseling groups help make real this dimension of the doctrine of the church.

The Church as the Confessional Community. Historically, the people of God are a confessing people. They confess not only their faith but their departure from their faith—union with their God. We are a people created in the image of God and called to sonship. We are a people made holy by the redemptive work of Jesus Christ. But we are also a sinful people whose lives and relationships become broken, alienated, and guilt-laden. We hurt one another. We become punitive toward ourselves in attempts to expiate our guilt and to recover the love relationship lost.

Fortunately, expiation is already accomplished; atonement is already made. Intellectually, members of the congregation know this. Many do not know it existentially, in the emotional depths of their being. The problem becomes one of how to appropriate the atonement already made and how to experience the forgiveness of God already guaranteed to us.

Confession is the way by which we appropriate God's forgiveness and return to communion with Him. The confessional ministry is a major ministry of the church, but where can a person make confession in Protestant churches today? Many say that private confession is enough or that public confession is possible through the liturgy of worship. This sort of public confession, however, may not provide a structure in which to get at the concrete shape of one's sin. Often sins confessed do not touch the sin out of which basic guilt has had its source. Furthermore, general confession does not help one to acknowledge before others, "This is who I really am";

and to hear others respond, "We are more like you than different from you. We love you because we ourselves are loved by God for who we are." Each person, to be healed, needs to confess to a brother or brothers, as well as to God. The Apostle James admonishes:

> Is one of you ill? He should send for the elders of the congregation to pray over him and anoint him with oil in the name of the Lord. The prayer offered in faith will save the sick man, the Lord will raise him from bed, and any sins he may have committed will be forgiven. Therefore, confess your sins to one another, and then you will be healed.   James 5:13–16.[5]

The psychologist would say that each person needs to socialize that which is unacceptable—that which causes him to feel separated because he has broken faith with God and his community, whose acceptance he treasures. Another way to put it is that each person needs to be honest in his relationships in order to be authentic. Otherwise, he makes use of mechanisms of defense to conceal his real feelings and thoughts. He becomes false and hypocritical because he fears social rejection, or, because he seeks to avoid self-rejection, he masks his real feelings. Confession, hence, is the royal road to healing.

The counseling group in the church context provides a new wineskin through which to restore the confessional ministry and enable the church to become the confessional community. As a person makes confession of who he really is and how he really feels, and is heard and accepted, the chasm between who he is and what he ought to be is bridged. New energies are available for authentic living, and a way is opened up for faith's adventure in relationships with God and one's brethren.

Some resist group counseling because they resist sharing deeply personal things. The fact that a group moves from the social level to the confessional level makes it easier for members to open themselves and become honest before God and the community. Usually, one member has the need and/or courage to share his hidden feelings. Once one member has been able to take this leap of faith, a highway

[5] Quoted from The New English Bible (New Testament) © The Delegates of the Oxford University Press and The Syndics of the Cambridge University Press, 1961.

is opened up in the wilderness for others. Once one is given the gift of an honest, trusting relationship by another, he is enabled to come from behind the wall of his self-imprisonment into the freedom of fresh air and sunshine and "air out" his wounds, grief, hostility, and guilt.

The group may not call these experiences confessional moments. Nevertheless, the power of God is at work within these moments to cleanse and purify, to heal the cleavages within and without, and to restore persons to life-giving communion within the community of faith. At times the counselor acts as interpreter to enable the group to perceive what is happening from the perspective of faith.

The Church as the Caring, Healing Community. One of the cardinal concepts of the New Testament is the church as the Beloved Community. It is the *koinonia* of those in communion with the God who loves and of those who are in loving fellowship with one another. These are those who know the pain of death and separation, who once had no hope, were afar off and outside the commonwealth of faith, but who have been brought near in the blood of Christ (Ephesians 2:12–13).

The church, when it *is* the church, becomes the redemptive, loving, healing fellowship. If there is any place in the world where broken and estranged persons—persons who do not know who they are and Whose they are—can find themselves, the church should be that place. Here they should find a people capable of involving themselves in depth with other persons. This is possible because God Himself has plumbed the depths in His involvement in our existence. He has done this not only in Jesus of Nazareth, but He seeks to do this in and through the concrete, historical, contemporary Christian community.

The people of God try to love, but their words and acts often fall to the ground. They often have difficulty in being open, involved participants in the sufferings of others. This is because they cannot be open to and participate in their own suffering and/or let others participate in it with them. Their words and relationships often fail to communicate to another, "You are loved." The following group session discloses this in a poignant way. Ann had just described her lifelong sense of cut-offness from members of her parental family. She then exclaims:

Ann: I am just sick and tired of all this mess. I'm sorry, but it just has to come out of me, I guess. I just feel that we yak, yak, yak about love around this place and all I see expressed is hate. I can't see where love is . . . what is called love is, as far as I can see it, hate. Now this is exactly what goes on here. It is denying your personal existence. To hell with you! I don't think you exist. This is how I feel. And I am fed up with trying to pretend it is love.

Richard: I can appreciate how you feel.

Arnold: I think what you ought to do is to try the power of positive thinking.

Ann: Ah, hell, Arnold. I've spent hours and hours of positive thinking.

Arnold: Well, I think you might try prayer.

Ann: You are just like my father, who always said, "Go some place and pray."

Madeline: I can feel with Ann the importance of being who we are and to be recognized for who we are. I feel that is what we are seeking to do with each other in this group.

Tom: I can understand how you feel, Ann. My wife often feels this exact way. I feel smothered about doing anything except to listen and intellectualize. (Exasperated)

Ann: Do I threaten people?

Tom: No, no, no. I wish I could get . . . I do feel . . . My approach to your problem is to intellectualize, to try to explain your problem. But it's not going to be explained. It's going to be somebody . . . it's going to be all of us to feel this. It's not going to be talk.

Ann: I don't think it's going to be talk either. I think conversation leads to relating but somehow relating isn't taking place and this is the essential thing.

Counselor: Yes. What I feel Ann is asking for is not an intellectual answer to an academic question. I think Tom senses what Ann's real question is. The real question is, "Does anyone care?" Ann may have experienced more of a real answer if a group member had reached

out and taken her by the hand. The answer would
have come and not a mumbling word would have been
spoken.

"Conversation may lead to relating, but relating is the essential
thing." Ann brings judgment to the church that talks about love
but is loveless as it talks. To advise, to seek to explain is not bread
to the one who hungers simply to know that someone cares. The
counseling group is the church to Ann at this point. Through processes such as these, members grow in the capacity to give and receive love. As this happens, the counseling group takes on the shape
of Christ's *koinonia*.

Group Counseling and the Nature of the Ministry

James D. Smart delineates four operational aspects of the ministry
of Jesus Christ, which he affirms is the ministry of the church. The
ministry of Jesus is a kingly, prophetic, teaching, and priestly ministry.[6] Group counseling is primarily priestly and pastoral.

Group Counseling and the Priestly Ministry. The priest in
the Old Testament had the primary function of mediation between
a holy God and a sinful people; he offered sacrifices for the people's
sins. For Christians, Jesus has made sacrifice once for all. Hence, in
most Protestant communions, ministers are called pastors instead of
priests. They seek to give tender, loving care to a person or to small
groups. In this ministry to people in need, they seek to be instruments through whom God may act and to make available individual-
ized support, guidance, and reconciliation. Other operations of the
ministry are present in group counseling, but in a less focal way.

Other Offices of the Ministry. The *kingly or administrative
function* appears as the counselor and the group establish their
covenant and standard operating procedures. If fees are charged,
they provide one way to measure a member's commitment to and involvement in the group. Payment of fees often reflects response-
ability—the capacity to respond and commit oneself to the process
of counseling. At times, the counselor will call into question financial
negligence in order to clarify a member's motivation for counseling.

Group members also have a way of disciplining one another. One

[6] *The Rebirth of Ministry* (Philadelphia: Westminster Press, 1960).

member informed the group that another member had broken the covenant of confidentiality. The offender was called on the carpet and the group reaffirmed together this discipline of their common life. Another such instance arises when a member is consistently late. At first the group will "look the other way" but eventually will call this act into question.

The counselor and members take prophetic roles at times. This forth-telling happens in confrontations in which the value systems of group members clash. For example, the member who acts out, who monopolizes attention, or is manipulative, superior, and dominating will eventually be brought low by fellow members. A group grows in its ability to value a person as a person and to resist the depersonalization of another when he is treated as a thing. A member or the counselor often interprets the religious meaning of such prophetic encounters as follows: One member was talking about how burdened she was with all she felt she had to do. Luther remarked, "We often weigh ourselves down. There are demands and needs we have to respond to, but often I am the one who overloads myself. I think you do this, Emily."

Emily admitted this was so. Discussion followed up this theme and at the close of the hour the counselor commented, "I recall words like these, 'Come unto me, all who are overburdened and I will give you rest. Take my yoke on you and learn of me, for I have a correct estimate of who I am and what I can do, and I will give you rest.'"

Finally, group counseling becomes a *teaching* group in two respects. Members do teach each other. They bring their wisdom and insight to the group. The counselor also becomes an interpreter and teacher. He makes available his wisdom gained from experience and from his studies of theology and the behavioral sciences. He is careful, as any good teacher is, however, to time his insight to the readiness of the group to appropriate it in terms of their own present experience in the group.

In the second place, a counseling group is a school for training the laity for their own priestly or pastoral ministry. Group members are learning to be instruments of healing and reconciliation. They transfer their learning and practice to their interpersonal worlds of job, church, home, and neighborhood. They become disciplined in the art of listening and responding in a helping way. Thus priestly, kingly, prophetic, and teaching operations of the ministry are all present in a counseling group. But of primary significance is the rediscovery that the church's ministry is the work of the entire people of God—laity as well as professional ministers. The priesthood of all believers becomes actual fact as members, with the help of the pastoral counselor, minister to one another and eventually to those without the camp.

The writer has by now communicated his enthusiastic conviction that group counseling is integral to the church and its ministry. A sober word, however, is in order. No one method can fulfill adequately the ministry of the church. Nor can a counseling group be the whole church. A counseling group is not called together to worship. The church is. The counseling group may be the only church some members have or know, but this group has a limited and specific purpose, namely healing.

In the age of specialization within the ministry, the danger exists that overemphasis will be given to one office of the ministry. When this happens, the ministry is truncated and fragmented and its unity lost. The pastoral ministry, whether individual, family or group care or counseling, may be midwife in the birth of souls. The spiritual infant, adolescent, or mature man, however, needs the nurture and challenge of the ministry of Christ in its unity and wholeness. The author is amazed as he observes ways in which the worship service and the proclaimed word complement the word experienced in the relationships within the counseling group. The "language of the preached word" and the "language of group relationship" deepen both experiences for the believer and enable him to hear, to understand, and to obey.

CHAPTER THREE

The PASTOR As A GROUP COUNSELOR

What is the image of the pastor in his role as a group counselor? What are the gifts, training, knowledge, and skills that contribute to effective leadership of a counseling group? How do his role and participation enable a group to become a healing group?

The Pastor's Preparation

The field of group psychotherapy and group counseling is as yet young. Most professional group therapists are self-taught; they are mainly psychiatrists, psychologists, and social workers who have extended their individual counseling practices to include the counseling of persons in groups. A few now devote their entire practice to group psychotherapy. In most cases, the pastor who becomes a group counselor has had no formal training or supervision for this task. Just what skills does his previous pastoral experience afford and what further preparation will he find helpful?

Previous Counseling Experience. The pastor's previous counseling experience with individuals provides an indispensable backlog of training in forming empathetic supportive relationships which give security for the anxious and fearful parishioner. In those experiences he has "worked through" some of his own anxiety and has come to know that he cannot solve another person's problem. Rather, he learns that he can be "with" the other person, hear him out, clarify and interpret his communications, explore new ways of understanding and possible alternative ways of responding to his problem situation. These same attitudes and acts of the counselor are also functions of the counseling group as a whole. The pastor becomes the agent who enables group members to perform these functions for each other. He uses his understanding of how counseling works to teach and train the group to be counselor to its members.

Previous Group Leadership. The pastor will have had experience as a leader of groups; in fact, this is his primary role—he leads the entire congregation and shepherds many types of small groups. He has learned how to attend to each person in the group, how to elicit participation from each member, how to help reconcile differences, and how to keep the group focused on its task and goal. In fact, supervisors in training centers frequently note that ministers are gifted in human relations skills in comparison with trainees in other professions.

In various functions of his ministry, the pastor plays an authority role. As proclaimer of the Word of God, he is at times tender, compassionate, and supportive. At other times his authority takes the stance of teaching, persuasion, exhortation, confrontation, and disciplinary concern. He represents the God who in love nurtures and supports; he also seeks to represent the God who in love calls to obedience to his will.

Any studies which get at effective leadership will profit the pastoral group counselor. The two types of leadership relevant in group counseling are the authoritarian and the democratic.[1] The authoritarian leader makes for a leader-centered group. He determines policy, methods, and goal of the group, and member responsibilities. He criticizes and praises but is aloof from group participation. Comparative results show that more tension, hostility, and group instability develop in autocratically led groups.

In contrast, the democratic leader is group-centered. He elicits contributions from group members and enables them to perform the functions enumerated above. Groups that are democratically led develop more cooperative endeavor, constructiveness, a sense of communion, objectivity, and stability.

Helen I. Driver has analyzed 11 typical responses of group leaders: (1) silence, (2) hmm, (3) reflection, (4) clarification, (5) interpretation, (6) information, (7) suggestions, (8) advice, (9) orders, (10) threats, (11) coercion. She observes that group-centered leader responses fall under categories 1 to 5. Responses of directive leaders fall under categories 6 to 11.[2]

[1] Kurt Lewin and Ronald Lippitt, *An Experimental Approach to the Study of Autocracy and Democracy, Small Groups: Studies in Social Interaction;* edited by Paul Hare, *et al.* (New York: Alfred A. Knopf, 1955), p. 516 ff.

[2] *Counseling and Learning Through Small Group Discussion* (Madison, Wisconsin: Monona Publications, 1958), p. 95.

Should the pastor, as a group counselor, be directive or group-centered? Later, ideal personal qualities and role functions of the counselor will be discussed, but at this point, experience in counselor training underscores the importance of each counselor being *who he is and playing the role that is natural for him*. The pastor who is aggressive will likely be more directive and vice versa. Generally speaking, when the counselor is comfortable with being himself, he is less anxious. This reduction of anxiety on the part of the counselor enables him to be more genuinely responsive and helpful.

This insight came clear in a case conference in which the writer and a psychiatrist gave supervision to a minister in clinical training who had been assigned as a group counselor. He expressed his anxiety over his new assignment: "I know I have a tendency to talk too much and to give too many interpretations. In the last session I tried not to talk but I did not feel right in the group." The psychiatrist replied, "Go ahead and act naturally in the beginning. If your participation hinders the progress of the group, you can take steps to modify your actions. If you try not to make a mistake and hold yourself aloof from the group when it is natural for you to involve yourself, then you have no basis upon which to evaluate and learn from your experience."

Continuing Education. There are several ways the pastoral group counselor can increase his competence. He can avail himself of an increasing body of literature on group theory, group leadership, and group therapy. Several significant books are listed in the bibliography. He also may wish to subscribe to the journal, *Group Psychotherapy*.[3]

Workshops in group dynamics offer training in skills and understanding of leadership. Such workshops are held at different times and places in the United States; information is available from the National Training Laboratories, 1201 16th Street, NW, Washington 36, D.C. The Episcopal Church has appropriated the skills of group dynamics as a part of its leadership training program. Laboratories are held throughout the country at various times in the year. Information may be obtained from the Department of Christian Education, Episcopal Church Center, 815 Second Ave., New York 17, N.Y.

Some pastors take six to twelve weeks away from their parishes or

[3] Beacon House, Inc., Box 311, Beacon, New York.

congregations and enroll in clinical pastoral education courses. Supervised experiences in pastoral care and counseling increase the pastor's awareness of his own personhood and his effectiveness in interpersonal ministry. Each year the January issue of *Pastoral Psychology*[4] details places of training.

A fourth source of further training is open to pastors in metropolitan areas where group psychotherapy is available. One of the best ways to learn the art of group counseling is to become a member of a counseling group oneself. In this experience, one gains insight into his own interpersonal functioning and also is able to observe an expert group counselor at work.

Time and/or finances may prohibit the options of clinical pastoral education or personal group therapy. A fifth alternative may be practical. An excellent way of training is to make use of the consultative services of a trained therapist who will give supervision to the pastor through conferences with him about the pastor's counseling sessions. Perhaps the cost of this service can be included in the annual church budget or may be volunteered by a therapist interested in an interdisciplinary approach to healing. When such consultation is out of the question, pastors can get together, as a small group, on a regular basis to discuss their counseling work in "pastoral case conferences."

The Pastor's Personality

The statement that counselors are born and not made has truth in it. In our time much stress is placed on the need for a scientific understanding and treatment of the ill person. The understanding of personality and the processes by which persons are made whole is one of the gifts of behavioral science to this generation. Counseling is enlightened and facilitated by this scientific understanding.

But counseling is also an art—one which can in part be learned but in part is given to certain individuals. This does not surprise one who is familiar with the witness of the New Testament and its teaching on gifts of the Spirit. Some individuals unconsciously are healing personalities; they exert a healing influence of which they may be unaware. Such persons become more aware of their gifts in

[4] Pastoral Psychology Press, Manhasset, New York.

the process of training, which enables them to employ the gift intelligently. The therapeutic personality may be characterized thusly:

Empathy. They are *empathetic*. They are sensitive to other people's feelings and thoughts. They can get into the world of experience of the other; they can identify, feel with, and live into the lives of other persons. They communicate this sense of "being with" the other person in verbal and nonverbal ways. Although they participate, they do not overidentify and get lost in the feeling experiences of others; rather, they are participant observers. They maintain their own integrity and identify in experiences of involvement. Raymond J. Corsini writes, "The ideal therapist is a warm person with a genuine liking for people, who really wants to see them improve."[5] Warmth grows out of caring for the other person, respecting him, and wanting for him the opportunity to realize more mature selfhood with its freedom for decision and commitment.

Patience. The successful counselor is *patient* and does not judge the merits of his work in terms of therapeutic success or failure. Every counselor takes delight in the emotional and spiritual growth of his people, but an excessive need to succeed becomes an expectation which the counselee overreacts to with compliance or resistance. In short, the successful counselor has a high tolerance for spending long hours which may or may not bear fruit.

Flexibility and Spontaneity. The effective counselor *can modify his tactics* and is not rigid, dogmatic, or unbending. At times, he may be group-centered, responding out of the context and content of what is going on in the group. But he is also in touch with his own world of feelings, values, and thoughts. He can make his own feelings and insights available to the group.

For example, a group had great difficulty "getting with" a crisis situation of one of its members. They wanted to talk about God, prayer, and the current crisis in race relations. Finally the counselor came in to say, "I feel that we are turning to topics which are generalized, and emotionally removed from Jan's crisis situation. I wonder if this means that we are quite anxious about her crisis and are having difficulty facing it with her." Here the counselor attends not only to what is going on in the group but follows the cue given by his own feelings that the group is being evasive.

[5] *Methods of Group Counseling* (New York: McGraw-Hill Book Co., Inc., 1957), p. 125.

Honesty and Integrity. Of other characteristics of a therapeutic personality that might be enumerated, those most significant are *honesty* and *integrity*. Description of some of the above-named qualities may falsely give the impression that the group counselor is a warmed-up jelly fish. But the effective counselor is committed to basic principles and values which do not change, although tactics may. Better to say he is committed to be with, respond to, and stay with his group in the way he feels will offer the best help. At times this incurs hostility from group members, if he does not permit himself to be transformed into the person the group wants him to be.

To illustrate: Frank constantly sought to get the counselor to be like a father who would approve or disapprove his plans. Finally his hostility broke forth: "When are you going to meet me man to man and tell me what you really think? You can never get a 'yes' or a 'no' out of this man!" The counselor did not yield to this pressure but asked if Frank was not asking him to accept responsibility for the decision.

At times the group or a member of it may make the counselor angry. He is human, too. If someone senses this and brings it up, the counselor owns up to it. He may tell the group that he is or was angry, and why he became so. The group respects such honesty. Their own anxiety and guilt over being hostile is lowered when they discover that the model of health in the group, the counselor, can become angry and not be destroyed by his own or the group's anger and hostility. The pastoral counselor seeks to become aware of his own transference reactions and to face these in himself with honesty.

This does not mean, however, that the counselor uses the group to deal with his own problems. Time given to this would divert members from the difficult task of facing their own situations. They also need, in the counselor, strength to enable them to stay focused on their therapeutic task. Often a group member will turn to the counselor with a question such as, "I wonder how you get along in your own family. Will you tell us about yourself?" At this point the leader replies, "I think my task is to serve the group, not to use the group to deal with my own problems in the group. I wonder why you asked this question." This moves the focus back to the inquiring member and the group to whom the counselor is committed to minister.

The Pastor's Task

A clear perception of his responsibility enables the counselor to move with a sense of purpose and sureness which reduces personal and group frustration to a minimum. His philosophy of leadership also determines his methods. The writer's personal experience, plus studies on group leadership, underscores the effectiveness of group-centered leadership (as against authoritarian) for the pastoral group counselor. As before stated, *the role and task of the counselor is to assist the group in such a way as to allow it to function as counselor of its members.* He does not assume responsibility for the healing of each member, but believes that this is the function of the group. His strategy can be spelled out thusly:

1. *The counselor leads group members to look to one another as the source of help.* In a newly formed group, members at first address and look at the counselor and seem to expect him to make a response. The counselor is a member of the group and responses from him are appropriate, but his nonverbal behavior will teach members to look to each other. Group counseling does not consist of counseling an individual in the context of the group, although some members will seek an exclusive relationship that invites the counselor to "give private counseling" in a group setting.

2. *The counselor focuses on the function of the group as a whole.* The pastor does not avoid "eyeball-to-eyeball" contact; he gives careful attention to what any person says or does but at the same time stays in touch with actions and responses of all members of the group. As he attends to the behavior of all group members, the person talking also begins to look around the group to find a hearer. This shift from counselor to group creates an opening to which any member of the group can respond. Persistent members direct not only their gaze but their questions to the counselor. At this point, the counselor may choose to recognize the questioner but to direct the question to the group. This strategy will link members to one another and will facilitate awareness of what is going on in the group as a whole. The counselor's focus is more than a technique; it represents his shepherding of the whole flock and of members in particular. Members learn to observe both verbal and nonverbal responses others make to an individual's communication. They stay in

touch with the entire interaction process and help each other to verbalize what happens in the group as a whole.

3. *The task of leadership of a group is a shared task.* The group counselor identifies with John the Baptist. He is a forerunner whose declaration is, "He must increase but I must decrease." We believe that the Holy Spirit is present and at work in a group committed to a ministry of healing in Christ's name. We believe that Christ is present in the community of the Holy Spirit. Christ becomes identified with and participant in His community. The Holy Spirit is that "wind of God who blows where he wills" to continue the work of Christ. Each member of the group, therefore, is a potential instrument of the Holy Spirit—the Advocate who comforts, confronts, and teaches. Leadership in a counseling group is therefore an emergent leadership,[6] to use Thomas Gordon's term.

The counselor never knows what is going to happen next, or who will initiate action and emerge as leader and counselor. Surprises are not uncommon. For example, the least participative member of the group may move the group to a new depth through the sharing of a problem. One group was spinning its wheels intellectualizing and advising. Finally a nonparticipant member interrupted and with tears said, "I want to do one thing before this group is over today. I want to tell you I feel that I cannot care about or love anybody in this group or outside of it. Furthermore, I am scared to death to let anybody know me as I really am." Within a moment the whole emotional climate of the group changed and it returned to its task of getting with another in an emotionally significant way. Various members could or had experienced feelings like this, and out of transactions that followed, one or more members emerged as leaders for each act in the drama of the group session.

4. *Each member has a contribution to make and the pastoral group counselor sees that each member's potential contribution is recognized.* No member is insignificant, and anyone who is absent is missed. Each is vital to the structure and economy of the interpersonal situation—the group is not the same if anyone is out. A person's worth is not measured by standard norms—popularity, success, or prestige. Actually, a person's best gift to the group is his real

[6] *Group Centered Leadership, A Way of Releasing Creative Power of Groups* (New York: Houghton Mifflin Co., 1955).

feelings, including those of fear, hurt, inadequacy, failure, and anger, as well as positive feelings of love, concern, and appreciation. When a person shares unacceptable feelings, he is surprised to find that those so difficult to share and that have meant devaluation of self are valued by others in a completely different light.

A nod of the head on the part of the counselor acknowledges the contribution each person makes, but more than a nod is often needed. The person may need the counselor to call his contribution to the attention of the group, which has ignored or overlooked it. More aggressive members tend to monopolize the stage and the less aggressive ones may have difficulty "getting in" the process. The counselor does not assume total responsibility for creating an opening for the silent one; this is a problem for both the nonparticipant and the group. But at points the counselor turns to silent members and asks for their understanding or feelings about what has transpired in significant encounters. Counselor action here communicates, "You are involved, though silent; your observations and thoughts are meaningful to us."

5. *The pastoral group counselor facilitates work of the group by asking for the relating of concrete personal experiences and the feelings that went with them.* Dead level abstractions will kill a group. They are not self-revelatory except to prove that the person uses intellectualization as "fig leaves" to avoid emotional involvement. Some group members will socialize, psychologize, philosophize, and theologize, but if they talk about their experiences at all they refer to them with all the pronouns except those of the first person— "I." The counselor helps each to personalize. For example, a person may really be talking about himself but he will say, "One feels thus and so, you feel this, we feel that; people generally experience things this way." The counselor simply asks, "I wonder, Henry, if you are talking about yourself and how you feel." Henry replies, "Yes," and the counselor suggests, "I wonder if you would note this for us by using the first personal pronoun, 'I'?"

A group stalemates when it gets off into an intellectual discussion and advises and theorizes. The counselor alerts the group to what it is doing. He may also comment, "I have a feeling that we are getting far removed from our feeling experience." He may also ask the group to explore reasons for its sidestepping. Leadership like this calls the group back to its difficult but needful task of dealing with the binding emotions which prevent self-realization within the context of community.

6. *The counselor helps the group direct its attention to immediate experience in the group and to problems within each member.* Existential analysis refers to *mitwelt*, the interpersonal world, and *eigenwelt*, the world within the self. The healing process moves in depth as members deal with the immediate spontaneous feelings of these two worlds. Members share their personal and social history. They talk about current problems with parents, marital partners, children, or friends. This gives others a "feeling for" and an appreciation of the nature of one's over-all problem situation. Such information is like the envelope on the letter; later, the time comes when members call each other into direct dialogue and encounter. One will say to another, "Phil, you have consistently talked about your wife's problem. I can see how her problems bother you. But you have not discussed your own difficulties. Your wife is not in this group and we cannot help her. You are in this group. I wish you would tell us for a change what your problem is, not what you think your wife's problem is." In such an instance, a member helps his neighbor explore "the log in his own eye" and calls attention to the need of each member to use the group for personal growth.

Therapy takes place in encounters in the immediate therapeutic situation. Had Phil continued to blame his wife, he may never have faced his own need for change and growth. Challenged, he began to respond to those within the room rather than narrate about "another outside the door."

Such action calling Phil to involvement is neither repressive nor rejecting. The group hears out the grief of another, but eventually calls upon him to search and share his own soul, and then he exposes himself to corrective experiences. In Phil's case, a female member identified with Phil's wife and interpreted how his wife must react to him. Phil was able to hear and use what the "wife substitute" said, because he was not subjectively involved with her as he was with his own wife.

7. *The counselor helps maintain group morale.* If a group becomes too anxious, defeated, or confused, it loses its capacity to function. Group morale is sustained in several ways. One is to give recognition to positive feelings members have for the value of the group. Such expression gives validity to the process and creates expectancy of progress.

At times, group process grinds to a halt. Members withdraw and become silent. One or two valiantly struggle to carry on. Intellectualization mentioned above causes this. Next, a seemingly insoluble problem may create a high level of anxiety and sense of defeat. For example, a wife brings up her problem with a resistive teen-age child. The group pinpoints what seems to be an almost irrevocably broken relationship with her husband and becomes immobilized because the situation seems hopeless. Again, confusion as to the task or purpose of group counseling causes a loss of thrust.

How are these blockades breached? Often a way comes when the counselor identifies group feeling. Statements are helpful such as, "I get the feeling the group is frozen . . . immobilized . . . is stymied." Discussion of such feelings clears a path. Afterward, the pastor may diagnose the nature of the obstacle or lead the group in exploring its difficulty. "I wonder if you are feeling that Jane's problem seems insoluble and if you feel impotent to help her."

Frequently a member will ask, "I wonder what we are supposed to be doing here?" or, "How does a group work? I just can't see how our telling each other our problems has changed anything." This question causes the group itself to redefine its task.

Group morale is also threatened if too much hostility builds up. One member may take unfair advantage of another, either through a hostile or a manipulative maneuver. In early stages of group life, members try to be nice to one another, and as yet they lack freedom, insight, and strength to resist or cope with such behavior. Instead, they inwardly become very anxious and/or angry. When this hostility or anxiety cannot be expressed, the group acts like a ship setting all sails to the wind but at the same time dragging all available anchors. The counselor identifies feelings and their sources and hauls the anchors aboard so the group can navigate through the troubled waters.

8. *Finally, the counselor contributes to group cohesiveness by drawing its "communication map."* A group is like a family going on a trip which takes them over many roads, and they need roadmaps to identify the highways and changes en route. In 90 minutes, a group discusses many things; however, a counselor notes that discussion coheres around one or more "themes." Identification of major themes keeps the counselor and group from getting lost. This communication map of theme identification tells the group what significant areas of interpersonal relationships have been explored. Insight or

revelation come when events and their meanings are joined. Sometimes the counselor picks up each theme as the group finishes its exploration. He may employ a summary at the end of the session. Theme identification and interpretation are discussed in greater detail as we move to a consideration of methodology.

In summary, the successful pastor-counselor continues to learn from his experience, from recorded insight and wisdom of others, and from opportunities for specialized training. He appreciates the importance of his personality in the healing process and evaluates his gifts and limits. Furthermore, he seeks to fulfill his role of enabling the group to make use of its own resources in the healing task.

Part II

THE FORMATION OF COUNSELING GROUPS

CHAPTER FOUR

PREPARATION Of The CHURCH

For COUNSELING GROUPS

The church invests much time and energy in each generation over the issue of orthodoxy—sound or correct teaching. This is important; good seed gives promise of an abundant harvest. Any wise farmer selects seed that passes a high germination test and has previously demonstrated high yield.

But quality seed is only part of successful farming. Jesus understood the significance of another factor—quality of the soil (Mark 4: 3–20). Seed falling on unplowed, rocky, weed-infested earth is not likely to bear fruit. The parable of the sower directs us to consider preparation of "the soil of the church" as essential to successful group counseling.

Attitudinal "Sets"

The success of the pastoral counselor may hinge upon the church's acceptance and support. The pastor's ministry is one the church gives him, and ordination invests him with an institutional role, status, and office. However, at the personal level, one cannot serve unless a ministry is given him by an individual or a group. Several attitudinal "sets" within the congregation may hinder the appropriation of the gift of the ministry of group counseling. If the people are prepared, his decision to follow this method is confirmed and sustained by the whole congregation.

Rediscovery of the Church's Healing Mission. The first stage of launch of group counseling may call for a re-examination of the healing mission of the church. Since the Reformation, the church has given its chief emphasis to communicating the gospel—preaching and teaching—and keeping its organizational structures intact.

But Christ's commission includes healing of the sick. On the whole, the healing mission of the church has been channeled through church-related hospitals and institutions. These agencies of mercy witness to Christ's care and concern for the sick.

Such efforts are commendable, yet this generation begins to ask with Jeremiah: "Is there no balm in Gilead; is there no physician there? Why then is not the health of the daughter of my people recovered?" (Jeremiah 8:22, KJV).

Jeremiah's question can be rephrased, "Is there no healing in the structures of the life of the gathered community?" The truth is that healing is potential in all the structures of the life of the church. In the words of Jesus, "Where two or three are gathered in my name, there am I in the midst of them" (Matthew 18:20 RSV). The context of this passage contains directions for a process of reconciliation with a brother guilty of an offense. The church is directed to move with conciliatory concern toward this brother. If he refuses to hear and become reconciled, the church acts with Christ's authority to discipline him.

Christ among us is the Christ who heals the sick, then and now. Through healing He bore witness that indeed the Kingdom of God had come in power in His own person. The New Testament supports the following affirmation:

> The redemption which God in Jesus Christ brings to the world is sufficient for the conquest of every evil. . . . We believe that the advent of Jesus Christ marks the beginning of the end of the Kingdom of evil. . . . Among the evils from which God in Christ is able to redeem man are the myriad forms of physical and mental illness. It is plainly the understanding of the New Testament that health in body, mind and spirit is the ultimate will of God. . . . The consistent attitude of Jesus Christ and the apostles toward illness is one of positive conquest. . . . The Church of Jesus Christ has a ministry to the sick which cannot be compartmentalized or delimited. Our ministry is not to "souls" in abstraction; our ministry is to men in their totality as creatures whose whole lives need to be filled with the power of God.[1]

Various churches today seek to rediscover this healing mission, an inherent thrust in the work of Christ and the early church. The

[1] *The Relation of Christian Faith to Health* (Philadelphia: United Presbyterian Church in U.S.A., 1956), p. 9.

writer belongs to a congregation that is developing neighborhood intercessory prayer and fellowship groups. One Sunday evening each month, persons come for a service of intercessory prayer for healing, and the worship service is structured with healing as a conscious focus; the ancient practice of laying on of hands with prayer for healing is used. In a recent service, those who came wrote their petitions on cards for the officiating minister. A glance at these cards reveals what great need exists among the people for God's healing from sin and sickness and for power to enable His people to take on the cost of discipleship.

Why discuss the need for a healing service in a book on group counseling? The point is this: Congregations that take seriously the command of Christ to be a community where God acts to heal are communities that welcome and support other approaches to healing. The church is more complete that includes the *charismatic* approach to healing as well as the *scientific*. Group counseling makes use of scientific insights and methods. This process has the advantage of enabling a person to gain in depth emotional insight into the concrete shape and nature of his sin or difficulty. This requires a period of time. The charismatic approach, on the other hand, operates in the aoristic tense. This is a *kairos* moment, a fullness of time in which God acts in a focal way. In this moment, a person's values become reoriented around the ultimate values—the love and forgiveness of God. In this moment, a person's loyalty becomes recentered in affirming anew the supremacy of the lordship of Jesus Christ. Anxiety and overpreoccupation with temporal concerns give way to "the expulsive power of a new affection"—seeking first the Kingdom of God. Many pastors today are concerned for a recovery and rediscovery of the healing potential in every congregation in which Christ dwells and where the concern to fulfill His healing purpose is a live one. The pastor who leads his people in this adventure of faith and practice will find a people responsive to opportunities opened up in group counseling.

The Congregation's Expectations of the Pastor. The congregation has its own expectations of the minister's responsibility, which may be far removed from a Biblical view and discrepant with the pastor's own expectations of himself. Recent studies of emotional illness among ministers indicate that tension stems from conflicts between these two sets of expectations. This conflict is similar to the struggle between marital partners when the husband assigns a role to his wife that she does not assume. For example, if he expects her to clean house twice a week but she is content to run the vacuum and dust every two weeks, trouble brews. The role he assigns her is not congruent with her own role expectations.

If the congregation does not see group counseling as a valid investment of the pastor's time, his counseling work suffers from critical reviews from members. A pastor in a large city had many requests for counseling appointments, but some members disparaged his counseling work and insisted he should do more pastoral visiting. Perhaps he should have. The real question is whether the pastor informs and clears his plans with his congregation. With one pastor, telling his congregation where and to what he feels God is leading him to give special attention is standard operating procedure. He requests his people to release him from other responsibilities and to give him prayer support.

Resistance to Group Counseling. Group counseling cannot be successfully conducted unless it is structured as such and unless persons involved are selected and prepared for this procedure. One minister attempted to employ group counseling methods in a seminar. The seminar was structured so that people could bring up their personal and religious problems. In these seminars, members were so accustomed to having a "topic" to discuss that none could participate except as they evolved a topic for each session and proceeded in the usual manner to attack it intellectually. Any attempt from the leader to elicit personal experience met with a solid wall of silence. When counseling takes place within the framework of already structured groups, it is more likely to be effective if a "prayer therapy" approach is adopted. (See page 60.)

Another stumbling block is the fear of exposure to those with whom one has social relationships. This problem is largely eliminated in groups conducted by a psychiatrist, where persons in the group are strangers to each other at the beginning and anonymity is maintained through the use of first names. In the church, group members are likely to know each other. They may fear that group confidences will become gossip as well as wonder if they can reveal their true selves to persons with whom they have frequent association. These two very real fears disappear as members learn to trust the covenant with each other. Their relationships outside the group begin to take on new depth and meaning, and word soon gets around that "counseling groups are great."

Preparatory Methods

Sermons. A series of sermons can prepare the congregation for group counseling. The pastor can do for his people what the writer seeks to do in this book. We have examined some meanings of the nature of the church and implications for healing, we have touched on the healing mission of the church, and we have looked briefly at the sociological dimensions of the nature of man. The pastor will be able to translate this social perspective into his theological understanding of man's misery and grandeur.

Advisory Committee. Another way to move at the grass-roots level is to involve several laymen in discussion and planning. The pastoral care committee or group concerned with visitation of the sick may be the logical group with whom the pastor can discuss his plans. Such a group helps clarify his interpretation before he presents it to the entire congregation. As he enlists the support and understanding of this group, they become interpreters to the church. The above suggestions grow out of the writer's background of ministry in a "free church" tradition. Pastors in episcopal and presbyterial systems of church government will have their own unique structures through which leadership is channeled.

Pilot Group. The above strategy is based on a *holistic* philosophy of relating the whole to the part, and calls for cultivation of the intellectual, emotional, and spiritual climate of the entire congregation as a prelude to beginning groups. An inductive method reverses this strategy and begins with a pilot experimental group and relates this part of the church to the whole body. The pastor on his own initiative may choose to experiment with group counseling and appropriate the experience with the group as a ground for interpreting this ministry in the church.

Counseling in Existing Church Groups. Often counseling is understood by laymen to be a procedure helpful only to individuals with serious conflicts. Such an understanding fails to comprehend the confrontation of each person from birth to death with need to grow in all spheres—intellectual, emotional, social, and spiritual. Historically, the church's and the pastor's task has been the care and nurture of souls. The church has a responsibility to surround each person in each stage of life and to give him a context of relationships in which to grow.

The unique thrust of the church from a mental health standpoint is a *preventive* ministry. Many people lose physical and emotional health and turn to the pastor for help. But the majority of church members are those of a wide range of ages who are the so-called "healthy" and do not manifest gross signs of disorder. Each lives under the call of God to move through the developmental task of each stage of growth from infancy to senior adulthood. The birthright of the church and the pastor is to minister to all the stages of growth. To be preoccupied and concerned primarily with the so-called "sick" may shift the pastor from the major task to a role that belongs to physicians and other healing professions.

An appropriate place to begin may be with groups already structured in the program of the church. Such structures usually represent age and/or sex groupings, and each has its own developmental problems as well as the demands of the immediate life situation of each member. For example, *teen-age groups* are in the midst of assimilating the impact of bodily changes of adolescence; working through dependency relationships with parents in their quest for autonomy and independence; developing status and position within social peer groups; relating to the other sex in the adventures of dating, courtship, engagement, and marriage; choosing a vocation; and coming to terms with the claims of Christ.

The universe of *young adults* is an equally expanding world—establishing a home, having children, balancing the budget, developing proficiency in one's vocation, and relating to the larger social and religious community. *Middle adulthood*, on the other hand, is a time when the expansive movement is curtailed and one is called to a movement in depth. Middle age is the time when "the deep calls unto the deep" (Psalm 42:7). During this period, the imperative need is for the integration of one's entire personality around "the secret center," which is the indwelling Christ. *Senior adulthood*, in contrast, calls for "the simplification of life," casting off the unnecessary baggage, enjoying those things that remain though the body perish.

The needs of the above groups suggest several types of counseling that can be done in groups already functioning. They would include counseling with teen-agers, premarital counseling, vocational counseling, marital and family counseling, counseling single persons, and counseling with senior adults.

Leadership Training. From time to time, the pastor may use group counseling methodology in groups specially structured to meet other needs. The need for leadership training in the church is a perennial one.

The effectiveness of the church's mission depends greatly on competent leadership. Often leadership training is limited to instruction in content and methodology, which fails to touch the interpersonal problems of leaders. Take, for instance, a church school teacher's group that met weekly to prepare themselves for their teaching ministry to children. This group of eight teachers experienced much difficulty in their life together; they found it almost impossible to remain task-oriented. Personal problems of members frequently were injected into the discussion and the direction of the group became diverted and confused. This group needed help with their own personal and interpersonal problems as preparation for their task of teaching and for their functioning together as a mission group of the church.

Spiritual Growth Groups. The pastor will discover also certain individuals who are undergoing experiences of spiritual renewal. These have grown up within the institutional church and have been faithful in attendance, but all at once the gospel they have heard from childhood begins to come alive and burn within them. They hunger for a deeper understanding of themselves and for a deeper relationship with Christ and His people. The regularly scheduled classes and organizational meetings do not feed them with a high protein diet of the word of God that they can assimilate and relate to their gnawing questions and needs within.

As the pastor looks as well to the fields within the church, white unto harvest, he sees the need among the laborers. He also becomes aware of his limits in time and energy to serve so great a need. With Christ, he can but pray for more helpers in so great a harvest.

Studies on mental health resources in the U.S. stress the importance of training persons among all professions and in all organizations for the work of prevention of mental illness. The medical and professional schools cannot educate enough psychiatrists, social workers, psychologists, or other counselors to cope with the growing mental health needs of the U.S. Policemen, school teachers, lawyers, neighbors, friends, in fact, every person has a significant role in the life of another—from a mental health standpoint.

How can the pastor do two things: (1) train church members for a ministry that is significant from the perspectives of spiritual growth and mental health, as well as (2) employ a procedure that is native and integral to the unique resources and life of the church?

Prayer Therapy and Group Counseling

Revival and renewal in the present day church is *microcosmic* rather than macrocosmic. Except for the Billy Graham crusades, mass revivalism fails to reach this generation. But let us take a look at the emergence of intercessory prayer cells, discipline and fellowship groups, and prayer therapy groups. These appear like manna from heaven to feed a hungry people in their wilderness wanderings. These groups spring up in all denominations; they often become the scattered or dispersed church at work in the neighborhood and the market place. Mothers get together in their homes to experience Christian community, to study, and to pray for each other as well as others.

A "house church" gathers on a midweek night, or businessmen meet at the local YMCA for similar purposes. Some of the groups find guidance and deepening self-understanding and relationships through a new method called *prayer therapy. This procedure may be the preferred one for the pastor who wishes to begin a counseling group but who functions best in groups with a more formal structure and a group limited in time to 12 to 15 weeks. Conservative churches are likely to approve and receive a method which makes use of the prayer meeting—an "old wineskin."* A third reason commends the prayer therapy approach—lay leaders can be taught to use it, so that the pastor extends his counseling ministry through his lay leadership whom he supervises.

Origin of Prayer Therapy. In 1951, William R. Parker, a psychologist and speech pathologist, and colleagues at Redlands University, conducted a unique experiment with 3 groups of 15 patients each. All participants received psychological testing. Members of Group I were treated with psychotherapy; Group II members were instructed to pray each night before retiring but were given no psychological insight or procedure for prayer. Group III experienced both psychotherapy and specific instructions as to method of prayer. Full details of prayer techniques are described in the book, *Prayer Can Change Your Life.* After nine months, psychological tests disclosed 65 per cent improvement in Group I, no significant improvement in Group II, and 72 per cent improvement in Group III. Parker concludes:

> Comparing these results, even cautious examiners admitted it seemed conclusive that Prayer Therapy was not only a most effective healing agent but that prayer properly understood might be the single most important tool in the reconstruction of man's personality.[2]

Spiritual Growth Tests. Several ministers in Burlingame, California, began to meet each Friday morning in 1954 for an hour to an hour-and-a-half to discuss their spiritual lives. They covenanted to be personal, to avoid argument and intellectual discussions, to pray daily for each other, and to set aside at least a half hour daily for prayer and meditation. This fellowship was a healing one for all members. In 1957, they associated themselves with Yokefellows, a movement initiated by Dr. Elton Trueblood. Trueblood sought to revive and make use of basic principles for spiritual growth used in the Moravian Band class meetings.

The Yokefellow Groups appropriated the research of Parker and St. Johns. An organization, "Yokefellow Associates," makes six standardized psychological tests available to any church group wishing to experiment with prayer therapy. A test is chosen that deals with the area of personality they wish to explore:

1. Initial Personality Inventory (Minnesota Multiphasic Personal Inventory).
2. Self-Discovery (California Test of Personality).
3. Human Relationships (Edwards Personal Preference Scale).
4. Test for Young People (California Test of Personality, Secondary).
5. Life Potential Test (California Psychological Inventory).
6. Self-Awareness (Johnson Temperament Analysis).

[2] William R. Parker and Elaine St. Johns, *Prayer Can Change Your Life: Experiments and Techniques in Prayer Therapy* (Englewood Cliffs, N.J.: Prentice-Hall, Inc., 1957), p. 34.

Dr. Parker and a minister, Cecil G. Osborne, have worked out *spiritual growth slips* based upon the tests. Slips contain test results plus specific prayer recommendations and guided readings. These slips are mailed in sealed envelopes every other week to the group leader for each group member. Slips are read in the group in one session and discussion extended into a second session. A prayer therapy session usually begins with prayer, allows a major portion of the time for reading and discussion of slips, and closes with 10 to 15 minutes of intercessory prayer for group members. Tests and a leader's handbook can be secured from Yokefellow Associates, 1430 Palm Drive, Burlingame, California. Cost ranges from $6 to $14, depending upon the test selected.

A similar plan is available from Birkman and Associates, 1625 South Main Street, Houston, Texas. Roger Birkman, an industrial psychologist, is also a committed Christian layman. A method devised originally for personnel guidance and placement in industry has been carefully refined, improved, and validated over more than a decade. This simple but practical test becomes a method to help each individual discover his *basic needs*, his *unique talents*, and his *typical behavior under stress*. The test is based on an analysis of traits and attitudes which in their special forms of combination describe unique gifts, needs, and limitations of persons tested.

The Birkman method is to be commended for its absence of psychological jargon—it is written in plain English. It has further advantages—it gives one a perspective of the type of occupational situation in which he will function most proficiently and securely, and thus is a significant instrument in vocational counseling. This instrument can also be invaluable to the pastor and his people as they train church members and place them in positions of service in the church. Birkman cites other uses: self-development, education, counseling with youth, premarital counseling, personal counseling, hiring and placement of key personnel, personnel research, and use in small groups.

The method is available to churches through a nonprofit corporation called Talent Sharing, Inc. The fee for the test is $35 per person, a part of which covers cost of scoring and part goes to the organization.

Limits of Prayer Therapy Method. The advantages of a prayer therapy plan have been discussed above: a means to help each to know himself and to share this knowledge with others; suggestions as to ways to engage together in prayer and study, possibility of moving at depth in a relatively short time; and a structure that is known to the church and that gives objective materials with which to work. But what are the limits of prayer therapy with its tests from the standpoint of group counseling? Why does the pastor need group counseling theory and methodology to undergird leadership of prayer therapy groups?

First, there is danger that the materials produced by Yokefellow Associates may be used as another version of "the power of positive thinking." A reading of Parker's book and review of recommendations on test slips can give the impression that this is another form of "works salvation," or pulling one's self up by the bootstraps of positive praying. The authors maintain that healing is an act of God. Much of the book deals with the "acts of man," but perhaps this grows out of the abundant enthusiasm the authors have for their discoveries.

A second limitation lies in the danger that group members gain intellectual insight and engage in intellectual discussion so that they fail to get the emotional insight growing out of interpersonal interaction and encounter in the group. Only emotional insight frees a person for decision and change. Otherwise, values from prayer therapy may be superficial and short-term.

Finally, although group leaders are given some instructions as to their leadership functions . . . prayer therapy materials do not as yet provide leaders with an adequate philosophy and methodology of leadership based upon group dynamics theory. Until the processes of group life are better communicated to leaders, prayer therapy groups may not reach the level of problem-solving and personal growth which is otherwise possible. For this reason, pastors who choose to do group counseling in the framework of a prayer therapy group will find their work clarified and deepened as they appropriate insights and methods coming from the field of group counseling.

CHAPTER FIVE

SELECTION *And* PREPARATION

Of GROUP MEMBERS

When forming a new group, the pastor may determine group composition and choose persons who will do each other good. How does he achieve a balance of personalities who interact therapeutically with each other? This is accomplished primarily through an initial exploratory and screening interview with each potential group member.

The Exploratory Interview

The initial pastoral interview has several purposes:

1. To create a secure, nonthreatening relationship that affords reduction of anxiety.

2. To elicit and respond to nonverbal, feeling communication as well as to the person's associative stream of ideas.

3. To bring into focus the "presenting problem" or what the counselee feels is his core difficulty or "chief complaint."

4. To determine personal motivation and attitude concerning counseling.

5. To assess strengths and liabilities for deciding what kind of counseling is required—supportive or insight, or whether referral is indicated.

The pastoral group counselor adds to this list a sixth concern: the choice of counseling method, whether individual or group. Usually, these things can be done in a one-hour interview. A second hour may be needed if counselees are very anxious or go into considerable detail.

Exploratory interviewing is an art—the art of being person-centered but at the same time securing a personal history, a part of the basis on which to evaluate individual needs and problems. The counselor begins with immediate concerns of the counselee. These feelings and ideas, when looked into, link the person with his total life experience —past, present, and anticipated future. All of life's experience is an interwoven fabric, though the counselee is not fully aware of the whole garment and does not see the seams of interconnecting parts. At times, the counselor explores in more detail one particular area of life, such as relationships with parents or spouse. Again the counselor enables the person to make transitions in order to relate other aspects of experience to previous ones discussed.

The personal history helps identify the *style of life,* to use an Adlerian phrase. It reveals *needs and goals* toward which one strives. It discloses *patterns of relationship* to authority figures, peers, and to those regarded as subordinates. It reveals *models* with whom one has identified and those rejected. The personal history also brings out the *concept of self* and one's feelings associated with this perceptual image. More accurately, it elicits the image associated with one's feelings about himself. This information is valuable for placement in a group, for counselor understanding, and interpretation of the member's participation in a group.

Although the pastor does not need full details (he can wait for a full picture to develop in the person's "time exposure" to the group), several items can be covered in the exploratory interview.

1. *Relationships in parental family.* Father's occupation and family's socio-economic status; client's image of each parent; how parents related to each other, to the counselee, and other siblings; how person related to each parent, and to his siblings and vice versa.

2. *Relationships to authorities, peers, and peer groups:* What successes and problems were encountered in relating to authority persons outside home, especially the teachers in public and church schools, the minister, and God? Did the individual develop close relationships with a few or several peers? What role —leader or follower—did one have in peer groups? When did person begin to date and how does he characterize developing relationship with the other sex?

3. *Relationships within marriage:* How does the person image himself and spouse within marriage? What are the ideas as to

masculine and feminine role responsibilities of each marital partner, especially regarding earning family income, care and discipline of children, tasks around the home, initiative in social and recreational events? How well does the couple communicate and hear each other and their children? To what extent can family members give emotional support to the needs and goal-striving of each? What are the ways in which hostility is expressed or concealment attempted? What are needs, fulfillment, and frustration experienced in the area of sex? What is the family's relationship to God and the church?

4. *Relationship to self:* How does one view himself—strengths and weaknesses? What are the person's assets—intellectually, emotionally, socially, and spiritually? Wherein does he experience a sense of loss, deprivation, failure, guilt, inferiority, and unacceptableness? To what does the person attribute these liabilities or how does he interpret their origin or cause?

The pastor does well to summarize information from the exploratory interview on a 5" x 8" card and indicate his prediction as to how counselee will relate in a group. Such a summary may look like this:

James Brown, 34, white, accountant, nominal Methodist, married 1½ years to Gloria, 29, no children; considering divorce, feels wife's emotional and sexual demands excessive, characterizes her as dominating and irritable most of time. Feels she rejects his mother and sisters. Jim unable to express his ideas and feelings, more recently has begun "to blow up." Wife has no other friends, unemployed outside of home, wants to talk from time he gets home, does not let him rest; husband developed mucous colitis condition six months after marriage; under medical treatment; father, deceased six years, a carpenter who had few friends; mother and women in family dominant; Jim attached to mother, never close to father, two younger sisters, closest to second sister. Marriage conflict began when wife resisted his mother's giving engagement party. On honeymoon, he retaliated by passive hostility in withdrawing and remaining silent. In interview tends to be dependent on counselor and asks for solutions from the counselor.

From such information, the pastor can predict that Jim will take a more passive dependent role in the group, that he will tend to withhold his feelings, and that his participation will be on an intellectual plane. A group can help him to become more aware and articulate of his feelings. His identification with more aggressive male members will give him a model for taking a more aggressive role in relation to both men and women. For a time he may tend to relate compliantly.

Criteria for Selection of Members

Suitable Candidates. Several therapists in collaboration published their findings on ideal subjects for group counseling.[1] The *shy* person who has not developed social skills will find best help in a group because there is less pressure on him than in individual counseling where he feels he must talk. The group gives him a permissive situation in which he cautiously begins to venture forth and gradually to gain confidence and competence in social relating.

In individual counseling, the dependent person is threatened and made to feel more guilty because of increased possibility of becoming trapped in helpless dependency on the counselor. In a group, dependency needs are met by one or two members and the person thus undergirded can move more affirmatively toward other members.

A third class, the *extremely deprived*, have some difficulty in a group but profit most from it in the long run. This person gets frustrated and at times hostile because he cannot have the exclusive attention of the counselor. In individual counseling and in a group, he will try to control the therapist and the group as a way of maintaining an exclusive bond. This is a desperate attempt to safeguard himself from further devastating deprivation. Group counseling helps to meet needs for attention, recognition, and love, but faces him with the reality that no one person can gratify all his needs. Trigant Burrow, a psychoanalyst, switched to group analysis because here

> . . . reactions were distributed over a group of people. . . . For it is only in the intangible reaction of several people, or many people together, that you can really get the loosening and breaking of the me-and-you contest . . .[2]

Parishioners who are out of touch or *unaware of emotions* and those who tend to *repress anger and hostility* are prime candidates.

[1] J. E. Neighbor, Margaret Beach, Donald T. Brown, David Kevin, and John S. Visher, "An Approach to the Selection of Patients for Group Therapy," *Group Psychotherapy and Group Function*, edited by Max Rosenbaum and Milton Berger (New York: Basic Books, Inc., 1963), pp. 413–422.

[2] D. H. Lawrence, "A New Theory of Neurosis," *loc. cit.*, p. 164.

The group gives priority to spontaneous expression of feelings. Members learn it is safe and acceptable to experience and communicate genuine feelings. Furthermore, group members register the impact of feeling which a given one communicates, though this one may consciously protest, "I really am not jealous or hurt." Out of group interaction, awareness of feeling emerges.

Others may not show characteristics of the inhibited, deprived, or oversocialized. Rather, they tend to be undersocialized, *to act out* feeling in behavior that creates crisis situations at home or at work. They seem to have no awareness of the way their own behavior complicates or contributes to relationship problems. They feel their needs and expectations are legitimate. The problem shoe is really on the foot of the other, they believe. A group serves to bring exploitative and manipulative behavior under its social searchlight and to represent social and religious reality.

Finally, individuals with *psychosomatic* complaints do fairly well in a group. Persons who somatize their conflict usually are highly resistive to relinquishing the "beloved symptom" as the explanation of emotional difficulty. They are less threatened by group than by individual counseling.

The above outline looks at potential members from the angle of their weaknesses or limitations. The ledger should show the following credits:

1. Some capacity to reveal oneself to a group of peers.
2. Potential ability to express aggression and tolerate hostility.
3. Neither great extreme of dependency or rejection in relation to authority.
4. At least average intelligence.

A person may come into the group with these strengths only in their potential form. Not all members are able to demonstrate such abilities in early weeks of the life of the group.

Unsuitable Candidates. The exploratory interview is the place to screen out those who cannot appropriate benefits of group counseling or who will either traumatize or block group function. Those with *insufficient contact with reality* are automatically excluded unless counseling is done in a hospital setting. A psychosis interferes both with reality orientation and with processes of communication meaningful to others.

Clients whose *behavior deviates* from the group norm require a group of their own and the services of a specialist. Here we need to distinguish behavior that is "ego-alien" from that which is "ego-syntonic." A group can accept, for example, the homosexual person who is struggling against these impulses, but it has great difficulty with the confirmed homosexual where this is preferred sexual behavior. Latent homosexual feelings and fears can be freely explored in a group. Sociopathic personalities and those with criminal behavior also are to be screened out. These delight in shocking the group with stories of deviant or illegal actions. "The lid is off their id." They are impulsive, exploitative, seductive, bent on immediate gratifications of their own needs and lacking in usual social restraints and courtesies.

The *incessant talker* disrupts a group. He uses excessive talk as a defense against disclosure of problems. He competes with the counselor for leadership of the group. Members grow hostile and spend their time listening to or resisting the chronic monopolist. As one member puts it:

> Jenny, I would like to help you but really I am very hostile to you. I feel that if we try to help you, none of us will ever get to deal with our problems. To tell the truth, you have been doing a lot of talking, but I really have no idea what your problems are.

Those with *suicidal, homicidal, or infanticidal impulses* stand in another category to be screened out. This would include persons whose self-destructive trends come out in a tendency to reveal bizarre and unacceptable content in the screening interview with the pastor. One such person who should have been screened out, left a group after six sessions. All of her communication centered around "How no-good I am," "I just am not worth anything to them," "My house is just a hopeless mess," etc.

Finally, the person in a *catastrophic stress situation* requires individual counseling or referral because his attention is focused on what is happening to him or within him. He cannot get out of himself enough to relate and be aware of the group situation. The acutely bereaved over death of a loved one or the loss of a marital partner in a divorce process illustrates. This especially applies to individuals who are acutely depressed and whose depression does not appreciably lift after consultation. Generally speaking, persons whom the pastor would normally refer to a specialist are those who are excluded from group counseling. In most instances, those whom the pastor himself would counsel individually are eligible to be in a group. The pastor would continue to give pastoral supportive care and guidance to the unsuitable candidates described above.

Group Composition

Prior to interviewing candidates, the pastor decides whether the group or groups should be homogeneous or heterogeneous in composition. This enables him to place members in a group that is balanced according to these principles of group formation.

Homogeneous Groups. These groups are organized on the basis of what members have in common. Groups may be composed entirely of men or of women. *Marital status*—single, married, divorced, or a parent without a partner—acts as another stackpole. *Age groupings,* for instance young adults, represent another alternative. A fourth arrangement takes a *common problem,* such as vocational unhappiness, into consideration.

Homogeneous groupings have the advantage of providing the ground of common interest. Because of similarity in the situations of each, the group usually has less difficulty getting under way. It suffers from limitations, however. It does not move to the depth and range of interaction that is typical of the heterogeneous group. The diversity in the latter provides a wider spread of member roles; learning is also facilitated because of a wider variety of experience among members. Paul's doctrine of the church as the Body of Christ with individual members possessing different gifts is highly instructive. The Body functions best as each member offers his unique gift to the unitive life and work of the Body.

Heterogeneous Groups. These are more cosmopolitan in character. The group counselor chooses persons who will complement each other and who may at times conflict with each other. For example, if he knows the spouse of a wife, he may choose a male member who approximates the husband's mode of relating. Heterogeneous groups are distinguished by a spread of ages, sex differences, individuals from different races and cultural backgrounds, and opposites in modes of relating.

This latter item merits special comment. A group will not function too well unless a few members—two to four, depending on group size—can fill leadership roles. Some balance is desirable between the aggressive and passive. One or two should have awareness of his anxiety, ability to communicate conflictual material, and sensitivity and insight into the problems and maneuvers of others.[3] Such members prime the proverbial pump and act as catalysts in the group.

One word of caution is due. Avoid radical extremes. To illustrate, ages should be within the 20- to 50-year range. Exceptions would be the more mature teen-ager or the older person who continues to search for creativity and freedom.

A further important principle is to provide homogeneity at the subgroup level. Ideally, each person should have at least one other member with whom he can identify and on whom he can count for support. At one point Evelyn said, "I don't believe I could stay in this group if Virginia were not a member." Virginia provided her with secure anchorage even though her experience in the group was stormy.

Husband-Wife Groups. Some ministers may wonder about the wisdom of placing husbands and wives in the same group. The *advantage* of this plan lies in opening lines of communication between marital pairs. A couple's attempts at problem-solving ends when they can no longer constructively explore their difficulties. They may continue to talk but talk is not synonymous with communication. The stance of each may be to defend the rightness and justice of his position but to find fault with the other.

Communication means sending a message that is heard, verified as to whether the proper meaning is received, and sending a response that takes into consideration not only one's own needs but the needs of the other. Counseling in a group setting calls upon other members to enable a couple like this to untangle crossed wires of their communication network and repair lines that have been broken. Placement of husbands and wives in the same group should be reserved for couples whose marriages are intact. They have marital stability that yields basic satisfactions and security. They can use *preventive group counseling* to work through minor conflict and to deepen their commitment and love to each other.

[3] *Ibid.*, p. 419.

The rationale for the above strategy is found in *disadvantages of joint marital group counseling*. When marriage is intensely conflictual, husbands and wives are placed in separate groups for several reasons:

1. Couples are more defensive in each other's presence. Neither wishes to admit to weakness or failure in the marriage for fear that admissions may be used as ammunition by the partner in subsequent battles. Furthermore, neither wishes the loss of face with other couples.

2. The more articulate and aggressive spouse tends to engage in verbal assault which calls forth and further entrenches the counterdefense system of his spouse (whether this be passive hostile relating—withdrawal into silence, weeping over hurt, threats to break off counseling, headaches, etc.)—or elicits a direct counterattack of hostile encounter.

3. Hostility ventilated in the group often supercharges the negativities of the relationship at home. The couple still have to live together once they leave a group session. When they are in separate groups, they ventilate their feeling and arrive home with a sense of release and clarification. As one member put it, "In these meetings I get rid of enough pressure so that I am beginning to feel like a human being through the week."

4. Finally, in a joint marital group, subgroups tend to develop on the basis of gender. Wives tend to subgroup in defense of women and husbands in defense of men.

Preparation of Group Members

The final five to ten minutes of the interview hour is devoted to interpretation of the value of group counseling, a brief description of what it is, what is involved in being a group member, and answering questions and securing consent for a group assignment. The following transcript suggests one approach to member preparation:

Interpretation of a Need

Counselor: Jim, we have spent the hour getting acquainted. You have been able to share with me something of the nature of the problem as you see it in relationship to

Gloria. We have covered briefly your personal pilgrimage prior to marriage. In the light of this, I want to recommend that you come into one of our counseling groups. Here others are working on problems similar to those you describe. (Silence)

Jim: (Hesitantly) I have heard about group counseling. I saw a demonstration on TV recently. . . . But I don't understand how people talking together solves anything. . . . Do you really think this would work in my case?

Interpretation of Group

Counselor: Yes, I think so. In fact, I think you stand to gain more from group than individual counseling. You have shared with me several things about yourself. You indicate difficulty in feeling at ease in social situations. You mention difficulty in developing close and meaningful friendships. Also, you have elaborated the difficulty in communicating ideas and feeling to your wife.

A counseling group gives one a context where it is safe to explore problems experienced in oneself and in interpersonal relationships. It is a small group of five to eight people. We purposely keep the group small. No one is under pressure to share until he feels he is ready to share. The fact that members share their common difficulties makes it easier for a new member. He soon discovers he is not alone; others are facing very similar problems.

Jim: Are people really able to talk about things like we have talked about this morning?

The Covenant

Counselor: Yes. The group members enter into a covenant with one another and agree that it is acceptable to share any kind of experiences. A counseling group is different from other social groups, where one seldom expresses what he truly feels or thinks. In a counseling group, we give priority to the privilege of *each* member's expressing spontaneously what he experiences in the group and out of the group.

This freedom is guaranteed by the group's covenant. Members covenant together that what is shared is property of the group. One is free to discuss what goes on in the group with another group member. One is free to discuss one's own problem or insight with a nongroup member but he does not seek to become an interpreter of another member. He allows other members to choose whether to reveal themselves to nonmembers and what to reveal. Let me add that significant conversations between members outside the group are reported in group sessions. This is a way of keeping all "in on" what transpires between members.

Jim: I think I could learn something in a situation like this, but I'm not sure what I can contribute. I think it would be more difficult to talk in a group than with you privately.

Member Contribution

Counselor: I think it would be a little more difficult for you at first. It is for most members. But usually after a session or two this feeling changes. It is difficult to describe how a group works; one has to be in it to appreciate its value.

The surprising thing about a group is that its values are different from other groups. Other groups place value on one's strengths and merits. But the most helpful and meaningful contribution in a counseling group is to share points at which one is having difficulty in his life. And even more significant is to say what one's feelings are. (Silence)

Jim: You have talked with Gloria. . . . Do you think she needs counseling too? Would we be in the same group? I don't think that would work. I have enough trouble trying to talk to her when we are alone.

Assignment of Spouse

Counselor: Yes, I have recommended that Gloria get into counseling also. Each of you has problems in relating which antedate your marriage and there are problems which grow out of your special relationship together. It is usually desirable that both husband and wife be involved because then each can work on his own difficulties which complicate marriage. I follow the policy of placing husbands and wives in separate groups. I feel it works best this way. (Pause)

Jim: When does this group meet?

Group Assignment

Counselor: A place is open in the Tuesday evening group which meets at seven o'clock. How does this time fit with your schedule?

Jim: This is a good time for me. (Pause) How long do you think I will need to be in counseling?

Counselor: The group is what we call an open group. This means that each member stays as long as he feels that the group ministers to him. We have a "leave taking" rule that when one plans to leave the group, he announces his plans and comes for one additional session so that others may participate in his leave-taking. Is that clear?

Jim: Yes, I believe so.

Major Decisions

Counselor: Jim, you mentioned you were at the point of considering divorce. We have one other discipline in group counseling. It is that no member shall make any major decision while he is a group member. There is a reason for this. At the present time or later in the group, you may be motivated by disappointment or anger to terminate your marriage. We believe that decisions made in times of emotional stress may obscure what one's real and ultimate wishes may be. After counseling, a person is in a position to make a more discriminating decision. (Pause)

Fees

Counselor: Jim, we have not talked yet about fees. The church has set a policy for the amount of $7.50 per person when two members of a family are in group counseling or $10 if only one is involved. What is your present financial position? (Pause)

Jim: I have a hospital bill for surgery about six months ago. We can afford this amount. It will press us a little but we can do it. (Silence) Does this mean we have one group meeting a week? That would be $7.50 a week for each of us.

Counselor: That's correct. (Silence)

Jim: How do we pay? At the end of each session or . . .

Counselor: My secretary usually sends out statements at the end of each month. Is this acceptable?

Jim: (Nods)

Counselor: A member is charged for each session whether he is present or not, except for two weeks of annual vacation. This is to say that each member has a place in the group that no other person can fill while he is absent. This makes counseling time different from individual appointments. Furthermore, it is to stress the importance of each person to the group. Every member is significant to the life of the group. When one member is absent, the group is different. There will be times members have to be out, but they are missed. (Pause)

Jim: (Nods) Am I to come this next Tuesday night?

Counselor: Yes, this is fine. (Pause)

Jim: Seven o'clock, did you say?

Counselor: Right. (Silence)

Jim: (Rising) Well, thanks for taking time to see me today.

Counselor: (Rising and walking with Jim to the door) I'll see you Tuesday evening then.

Jim: All right, I'll give it a try.

Counselor: (Nods and smiles. Lets Jim out the door and closes it)

Psychological Testing

Psychological tests are a helpful adjunct to counseling. They provide objective criteria that help the counselor check out his own observations and evaluations. Test results also may be placed in the hands of group members as one way to augment exploration of inner feelings and relationship patterns. The minister may avail himself of tests used by prayer therapy groups.[4] Such tests may be appropriated for both individual and group counseling.

Individuals may take tests after the exploratory interview if the pastor has requested them to reserve two hours for the exploratory interview. In most instances, tests can be administered with brief explanation at the beginning and without supervision by the pastor. Or, the pastor may prefer to wait and schedule time when the group as a whole fills in test forms.

The Question of Fees

At first glance, charging fees may seem out of character and out of order for the pastor and church commissioned to a ministry of witness and service to the world. Closer examination of policies shows that historically the church has charged fees for special services. Tuition is standard procedure for church-sponsored elementary, secondary, and college education. Church-related hospitals could not function unless patients bore major cost. Use of chapels for weddings of nonmembers usually requires a fee.

Special Services. Counseling is a time-consuming ministry that can be given to only a limited number. Pastors have scores of nonmembers who make claims upon his time and who assume no financial responsibility for the church's ministry. Perhaps members and nonmembers need to realize that this additional gift merits comparable financial response from them. Many pastors already invite nonmembers whom they counsel to make a "free will offering" to the church.

Therapeutic Value. The chief value of fees is their therapeutic value. A person who invests his money in counseling is motivated to use his time in a group to greater advantage. If he is not getting help, he makes this known and gives the group an opportunity to inquire what he expects and why he is not progressing. Or if the group begins to waste time on trivia, a member complains, "Look, I think we are fooling around. This is costing me ten bucks an hour. I want to get my money's worth." Fees also "set an end" in counseling. The nonpaying member may want to luxuriate interminably in the group climate.

In the third place, nonpayment, when fees are set, expresses the

[4] Cf., Chapter 4, pp. 61–63.

member's resistance to counseling. Delinquency may unveil hostility to the counselor or lack of motivation and resistance to the whole process.

Stewardship. Finally, fees bring into focus one's stewardship of money as well as time and opportunity. Certain individuals are chronically in debt. They spend more than they make. They confess they "just cannot handle money." Investigation of nonpayment of fees and other indebtedness may help to uncover helpless, dependent, receptive, masochistic needs of the debtor or aggressive exploitation by others. On the other hand, some are overly conscientious in the amount they wish to pay and quite anxious over any lapse in payment. Prompt payment may be a means of earning favor; their worth and value as a person may depend on it.

The counselor regularly goes over accounts. He brings nonpayment to the person's attention privately and makes this a means of therapeutic intervention. He encourages those having "budget trouble" or resistance over fees to make these concerns "grist" for the therapeutic mill of the group.

Amount of Fees. Some pastors use a sliding scale of $1 per session for each $100 gross income per month. Special reductions may be made for families who have several children or who support parents. In cases where income is very low, only a token payment or no payment at all may be appropriate.

A new profession is emerging within the ministry. Local congregations, groups of churches, and denominations sponsor 150 pastoral counseling centers in the United States. The number continues to grow at a rapid rate each year. This specialized ministry received national recognition in the birth of the American Association of Pastoral Counselors[5] in March of 1963. This organization seeks to provide fellowship, professional stimulation, and standards for the training of specialists in pastoral counseling. Many churches are adding ministers with such training to their staffs. The church may increasingly look to substantial fees as a means of supporting this specialized ministry.

[5] For information, write Frederick C. Kuether, Secretary, American Association of Pastoral Counselors, 201 East 19th Street, New York 3, N.Y.

CHAPTER SIX

The INITIAL MEETING

The time has come for the initial meeting. Two major tasks face the counselor and the group: (1) dealing with anticipatory anxiety of the members (who face a new learning situation) and their expectations of the counselor; and (2) ordering the life of the group—its structure and its direction.

Anticipatory Anxiety

As members look toward their first meeting, each may share common concerns, "What will the first session be like? This is all new. What am I getting into? I wonder how I will feel and act? Can I bare my soul to strangers and to friends? Will I be heard and accepted? Will all this really help me?" When a new group is being formed, members may have to wait two or three weeks until several others have been selected to form a core with which to begin. During this interim, anxiety may cause one or two to shrink back. They call the pastor on the phone. Then he must work through their anxiety with them.

Presession Counseling of Uncertain Members. Their anxiety takes on several shapes. Anticipatory anxiety over being in a group occasionally gets *displaced on finances*, if fees are charged. The person begins his telephone conversation with, "I've been thinking about being in this group. On second thought, I'm not sure my budget will stand it." The task of the pastor is to help evaluate the source of anxiety. He gives recognition that this represents an expenditure and that one must live within his resources. If he knows finances do not prohibit counseling, he inquires, "Helen, I wonder if it is the financial cost which bothers you most, or is it another kind of cost?" Astute persons turn to explore their underlying feelings of apprehension, otherwise the pastor may point up the real source of hesitancy. Discussion, followed with supportive interpretations concerning values of group counseling, usually is sufficient for the well-motivated person.

In a few instances, individuals may grow so apprehensive that coming into the group must be *postponed*. After a short time, particularly as they continue to experience their difficulties and as they hear success stories from enthusiastic group members, they call again and are ready to enter. Postponement may be avoided if the pastor promises to give short-term individual counseling in addition to group participation.

Certain counselees insist on *individual counseling* only. In some, anxiety causes them to become covertly or overtly controlling of the pastor. The unconscious wish to dictate is the basis on which they will seek healing. The pastor must then decide whether he has time for continued individual counseling—whether he yields to the person's defense and begins with him on his own ground. Ideally, he keeps such persons pointed toward a group, because what they most fear may be what they most need. They intuitively know they cannot control a group and that they will have to share the counselor with others. What some people most need is to be in a relationship that they cannot and eventually do not have to control.

In a church setting, word gets out as to who will be in a group. This may occasion a member's *request to be transferred* to another group if he does not like or has difficulty relating to one of those chosen. The pastor can point out the very fact of difficulty in relationship with this person is all the more reason to be in a group with him. In fact, these two may do each other and the group the most good.

Finally, the *poorly motivated*, having agreed to come in, call to announce their decision not to follow through. They are not genuinely interested in getting help, in personal change and growth. They have come to the pastor with the objective of having him get their mate to change, or "to solve their problem" for them, or they came because someone else pressured them—a parent, a spouse, or a court. In spite of their obvious need for help, the pastor can only let them follow their self-chosen way, if, after he has reasoned with them, they turn away. The problem is their problem and the pastor can only make himself available.

Getting Under Way. Those committed come to the first meeting with considerable apprehension, nevertheless. Usually the first meeting is "a success." Some people talk and laugh to relieve tension. The primary task of the pastor group counselor in the opening session is to release anticipatory anxiety in order to build morale and give members a beginning feeling of "it is good to be here." After introductions, participants may express how they feel about coming.

Counselor:	How did you all feel about coming this morning?
Rita:	Sort of strange.
Counselor:	Sort of strange? (Pause) Anyone else have that kind of feeling?
Annette:	Uh-huh, yes, uh-huh, I feel that way too. (Pause)
Greta:	I don't have strange feelings because I'm so interested in this kind of growth.
Gilbert:	(Quite affirmatively) Yeah, I don't feel strange either . . . I feel real eager in anticipation. I'm curious because I just feel kinda blacked out and at the same time perfectly fine. And the two are so inconsistent. I'm real curious to find out why things don't seem to mesh.
Counselor:	One part of you seems O.K. and the other part of you seems out of touch.
Gilbert:	Uh-huh. (Pause) I have a funny reaction right now that I may as well express. One of the things I've had most difficulty with is to always be surrounded by women. (Group laughs) I was raised as the only boy in a house full of women, and as an adult I still remain in a house full of women and my reactions are kind of negative to it.
Counselor:	And it has happened again! (Gilbert was the only male in the group at its inception)
Counselor:	Well, two of our members feel a sense of anticipation, and Gilbert brings a concern over disparate aspects of himself. He also has some feelings upon discovering he is the only male member at this time. (Pause) Two other members say they experience strange feelings.

(To Rita) What's this strange feeling like?

Rita: I think it is difficult to talk to you alone but with others here it makes it five times harder in one way. I really wonder if people are going to hear you.

Counselor: If *you* will be heard?

Greta: I must say something here. Your situation is the very antithesis of mine for I am seeking a group. I have no self-consciousness whatsoever and being in a group is easier than being with one person.

We see the counselor moving to help participants verbalize and ventilate their fears and resistances. Bach stresses that primary attention is given to emotional communication and release of feeling:

> Since the first meeting is consumed with alleviation of anticipatory anxiety, it follows that the content of communication is basically secondary to the emotional experience of extinguishing anxiety. These emotional dynamics of the very first meeting of a newly formed group illustrate a basic principle of group psychotherapy: Content of verbal communication is of secondary importance. The quality of emotional experience afforded to the participants is the main focus of interest for the therapist.[1]

Leader Dependence

The pastoral group counselor has a second hurdle in initial and subsequent meetings. In the first meeting he takes more initiative to help the group communicate fears and resistance associated with their new experience. As we shall see, he also takes part in determining group structure. These functions fill legitimate dependency needs for the leader to guide in this new adventure.

Participants, however, expect the leader to continue as helmsman—to be in control, to chart the direction, to give advice, to indicate approval or disapproval, to evaluate member performance as good or bad, and to defend or support special interests of participants. In keeping with leadership philosophy,[2] the counselor's effectiveness rests upon a shift of dependency on him by investing each member and the group as a whole with responsibility. Gradually he employs what is called "leadership by default." Rather than answer questions,

[1] *Op. cit.*, p. 37.
[2] Chapter 3, p. 45 ff.

which keeps him harnessed with group dependency, he turns questions back to the person and to the group. In other words, he abdicates the role of the lone source of wisdom and help. He calls upon each person's resources and resources of the whole group.

At first, the group may move slowly. Group tension may build up. Occasionally, a member appeals, "Dr. Thomas, what do you think? You are the authority here. Give us your opinion." This creates an opening to explore dependency on the leader and to point to the group as the source of help. "I notice that Greta continues to address me rather than other members of the group. I wonder why?" Members note that Greta seems to value the counselor's attention and comments more than others. Events such as these aid in the "transformation of motives" as members learn to share leadership responsibility. Once the group begins to function on its own, the leader is freed to initiate procedures that facilitate and deepen interaction and communication.

There are moments, however, when the counselor has difficulty in restraining himself. He may become anxious and feel a need "to get things moving." Or he may have "a brilliant insight" into the dynamics of a parishioner's problem. In other words, he may have difficulty abdicating. In one session, things were really "popping" and the counselor had great trouble containing himself. He kept saying to himself, in the words of Ernie Ford, "Keep your cotton picking hands off." Counseling, whether individual or group, calls for great patience, ability to wait and see. Another way to put it is that the counselor learns he is not the only one at work in the group. He comes to trust the group and the group process. More than that, he comes to trust the work of the Holy Spirit in the group. While attending what's going on, he silently prays for God to act and bring deliverance; to open eyes that do not see and ears that do not hear; and to set at liberty captives. Counselor anxiety is greatly reduced if, while he waits on the group, he also "waits upon the Lord."

Responsibility for Group Structure

Group structure consists of understanding and establishing group operating procedures and agreements. Herbert A. Thelen points out that "the group acts *as if* it operated within the spirit or letter of a set of agreements."[3] The pastoral group counselor helps the group come to an understanding of their formal agreements as to time, place of meeting, purpose, what can be shared, and so on. This raises the question of how much structuring the counselor does in the initial meeting. In a word, whose is the responsibility for establishing structure?

In the early days of group dynamics research, a leader came into a new group, sat down, and waited for the group to take initiative for group locomotion and direction. In other words, the leader delegated responsibility. This "leadership by default" represented a right-about-face corrective to an authoritarian type of leadership. It heralded the new awareness of powers and potentials within groups for creativity and self-determination. In addition, this philosophy of leadership positioned the leader as one who assisted the group in its own self-determination.

Counselor and group are involved in a common and mutual task and to leave the group completely responsible is to fail to meet legitimate dependency needs and expectations that the counselor function "as an expert." To dictate to the group invites resistance to that which is imposed from without, although such a use of authority may be asked for at first.

An either-or position fails to recognize that each group is different and its needs are different. Some groups delight in working out their formal agreements at the outset; other groups are frustrated. Their immediate concern is to deal with personal and group anxiety. They look to the counselor to help define structure so they can get on with urgent business of release from hurt and pain. The counselor, too, is not the same person in every group. Each group calls forth unique aspects of his personhood.

The experienced pastoral counselor has an over-all philosophy of leadership based upon his view of persons and how to help them grow. He does not, however, rigidly impose a theory of leadership upon a group. To do so is to image himself and the group in one way which says, "I have to be this way each time and the group has to be that way." Hopefully, we are in the process of image breaking, so that each can respond in a dialogue of I-Thou encounter: How the counselor responds and what role he takes depends in part on the

[3] *Dynamics of Groups at Work* (Chicago: University of Chicago Press, 1954), p. 297.

particular group he faces and upon what he feels and experiences in the moment. With one group, the counselor may simply sit in silence and wait for initiative from the group. On other occasions, he may take considerable initiative. The more passive and dependent groups may look to the counselor for more guidance and their need is valid. How to avoid getting caught in a dependency trap is the concern of the next chapter.

Establishing Group Structure

The Counseling Room. The place for a group meeting can be plain or fancy. A medium-size room, which comfortably accommodates eight to ten seated people will do; it may resemble a living room. Comfortable chairs should be arranged so that each person faces and can see others.

The pastor selects his chair and sits consistently in this position. Group members may change seats, but they recognize this one as the counselor's chair. The fixed position of the counselor is significant. How members seat themselves with reference to the counselor can be one measure of how they relate to authority. The most distant seat across from the counselor is often occupied by the person who keeps emotional distance from authority persons, who attacks at times but who wants the safety of intervening distance. The seat closest may be chosen by one who is more dependent on authority persons. Thus the dependent-rebellious polarity of the parent-child relationship is symbolized in the seating arrangement.

More often than not, persons with a more masculine orientation sit on the counselor's right and those with feminine traits sit on the left. How members sit in relation to each other is also worthy of note. Persons who engage in encounters with each other sit in opposite positions. Again, the safest position is to sit side by side; in-fighting may have its dangers but it is not as devastating as the fully delivered punch. The more orderly, regimented person is likely to choose the same chair each time. The "musical chairs" from session to session gives some indication as to how members relate to the counselor and each other. In charting movements of each individual's relationship in the group, changes in seating arrangements are revealing.

Time. The group should begin on time, whether or not all members are present. Time is an inescapable reality, equally important as space or the seating arrangement. Members eventually come to examine excessive needs for promptness and chronic lateness. A member in one group equated his habitual promptness with avoiding personal embarrassment and winning approval. Another saw her punctuality as a corrective to her mother's habitual lateness and inconsiderateness of others. Those consistently late and wanting the group "to fill them in" on what has happened before their arrival will find the group exploring cause of their tardiness. A group will uncover hostile and egoistic motivations. Time is one dimension of finitude; how each accepts, distorts, or denies it and why is a veritable therapeutic gold mine.

The pastor should arrive or admit members to the room only two or three minutes before the time of meeting. This diminishes the ever-present temptation to keep things on a social but emotionally neutral level. The pastor himself should be punctual—a group is likely to explore a counselor's lateness.

Introductions. At the beginning of the initial meeting, participants are introduced. First names are used. This form of address puts all members on the same personal and intimate level. It also provides anonymity for those unknown previously. Each person more fully identifies himself as he feels safe and secure enough to relinquish anonymity.

Identifying Group Purpose and Function. Frequently, in the initial session, a participant will inquire, "Why are we here?" This is especially true if the group contains those who are anxious without the safety of known structure. The counselor may ask members to give their own reason for involvement and understanding of how the group functions. Prestructuring done in the exploratory interview pays dividends; one or more participants are able to articulate a fairly accurate description.

Sometimes the counselor takes the initiative when interpretation can clarify or give support as participants experience fear and doubt over personal disclosures.

Counselor: I wonder what we are experiencing in this time of silence.

Annette: I feel on one hand scared to death and on the other hand very anxious for the group to begin and anxious to share problems and ideas and get some better thoughts on my own problems. I am not used to groups and [to Greta and Gilbert] I envy your easy ability to be with other people.

Counselor: It may be helpful to talk about what the group is and our purpose together. This kind of group is different from other groups. We have been trained from childhood how to act in social settings. We have been taught that one is approved if he acts in such and such a way and disapproved if he behaves otherwise. I think in this group we seek to be different in that we want to develop a climate or atmosphere where each person will have the freedom to be who he is within the moment—to say what we feel and think. The best gift we can give to each other is our own personal experience or our response to another member or situation in the group. We move on the premise that anything goes within the group as we cultivate spontaneity and freedom.

Here the counselor begins to educate participants as to the key task and climate. Much of his work in future meetings will be to help the group implement this chief element of structure.

Tape Recording of Sessions. A final element of structure revolves around whether to record sessions electronically, who decides about taping, and what use will be made of the tapes. Tapes can be of value both to the group and to the counselor, as interpreted in the initial meeting from which earlier sequences were cited.

Counselor: I think our time is about up for today. Uh, I have an idea that each of you feels there are "several untied strings" or "ruffled edges" that you wish could be ironed out. Or perhaps it would be nice to jump the whole distance in one hour and one-half session. (Group laughter) Uh, but there is time again next week and the week after that.

Before we go, let me bring up one further procedural matter. Some groups have chosen to tape sessions. There are several advantages. At times it is helpful to play through and listen to a part of the immediate or a previous session. This helps to objectify and clarify an event in group interaction. Also, when a member misses a session he may want to audit the meeting missed. Or, if one is deeply involved, he may find listening to the tape gives new understanding and perspective.

This privilege is possible only for a group member; no other person could make use of your tapes. Listening would need to be done here at the church. We could not circulate tapes. Tapes are confidential records for the benefit of the group.

There is one further advantage—research. We can improve our ministry if the counselor critically evaluates his leadership. I would find tapes a way to be more responsible to you as a group. Furthermore, I hope to share insight regarding leadership of counseling groups in a writing ministry. In this way, the group ministers to the church at large.

Taping is of no concern to a few. Others, after expressing their anxiety and hesitancy, affirm that it is a good idea. Occasionally, a person who engages in "classified" Government employment, such as the FBI or in diplomatic service, does not feel free to participate when sessions are taped. Although external reasons, such as one's employment, may prohibit recordings, resistance from others may be a symptom of suspiciousness and a lack of trust to be therapeutically explored—in other words, paranoid tendencies.

Some counselors proceed to tape meetings on the premise that this is standard operating procedure and that anxiety or acceptance of taping is a reflection of the counselor's anxiety or freedom. This generally is true. If the counselor feels comfortable, so will the group, although they may question the procedure and work through initial reservations. A group may be self-conscious at first, but they soon ignore and forget the recorder as they become involved in group proceedings.

Structure in Prayer Therapy Groups

The structure of the prayer therapy group is more simple. The initial meeting starts with prayer and moves to a discussion of what each person hopes to gain or achieve through participation. The leader may wish to give a brief account of how prayer therapy originated and some basic ideas which are articulated in Parker and St.

Johns' book, *Prayer Can Change Your Life*. The meeting is then closed with an intercessory prayer period and adjourned to take whatever test has been elected. Test results and discussion provide the backbone of structure for subsequent meetings, opened and closed with periods of prayer.

Leader and group members will profit if a period of silence is observed prior to each prayer period. Often prayer is rushed into with little opportunity for parishioners to "be still and know" God who is being addressed. Our activistic trend toward involvement leaves little opportunity for personal detachment and self-transcendence in which a person's spirit can ascend and look to one's wholly other, "the high and lofty One who inhabits eternity, whose name is Holy" (Isaiah 57:15, RSV).

Part III

DYNAMICS, PROCESS, AND LEADERSHIP

OF COUNSELING GROUPS

CHAPTER SEVEN

COUNSELING GROUP PROCESS

And DYNAMICS

The field of semantics and communication teaches us the importance of defining words. Definition of "process" is especially relevant in group therapy. It has two basic meanings: (1) act of proceeding; progress; advance. (2) a. Any phenomenon that shows a continuous change in time; as the process of growth. b. A series of actions or operations definitely conducing to an end . . . as, a process of making steel.[1]

The first meaning is the sense in which "process" is used in this chapter. We are concerned with the phases and stages of movement within a group, or the processes through which a group moves to reach its goal. The second meaning refers to methodology.

The word "dynamics" is also significant, and refers to forces that are active in a group to facilitate or impede its progress. Description of group process and dynamics is not easy. We are dealing with something alive and changing. Moreover, we are looking at several processes, all of which are going on at the same time. Description would be easier if we could hark back to a single cause-and-effect explanation—one causative factor produced such and such an end result. Exponents of *field theory*, however, show that any phenomenon demonstrates multifactorial causation and effects. In addition, *effects* become agents of further activity and change. To make this idea concrete, the group counselor is like the ringmaster of a five-ring circus with several different performances going on in each ring. However, in a group, each ring is not a separate entity; the rings are interlocking. For purposes of discussion, we separate out processes in several rings, which may be seen as follows:

[1] *Webster's Collegiate Dictionary* (Springfield, Mass.: G. C. Merriam Co., 1959), p. 672.

Movement in Each Group Session

A group meeting has a rhythmic ebb and flow; it is like a symphony in four parts or movements, each of which develops variations of the original theme. Like Tchaikovsky's "Pathetique," it may begin quietly, rise to a crescendo, then return to quietness again. But even before the first movement, the orchestra takes time to tune instruments and to warm up.

Group therapists have identified the *theme* as the *organizational unit* of a group meeting. A theme is a topic around which a group rallies. Each meeting may evolve one to four themes, such as (1) reactions to anger—fight or flight; (2) need for acceptance and difficulty of "taking up for oneself"; (3) ethics of salesmanship—use of pressure vs. respect for person (or problems of aggression vs. passivity).

The counselor can observe the following process connected with each theme:

1. Socializing and search for an emotionally significant theme or topic—the warm-up.
2. Rallying around a theme: group direction.
3. Theme exploration: group interaction.
4. Theme exhaustion: group satiety.
5. Search for a new theme.

The first phase is a time for reporting and communication of random thoughts. Reflections on previous meetings, events of the week, and inquiries as to each other's welfare are shared. Aimless conversation may continue or die down. In any case, group tension builds up. As yet, the group has no sense of direction or feeling of "getting with it." Some participants begin to show impatience. Then one asks to share a special concern or problem. Usually a given group session focuses initially around the problems of one person, and each person, sooner or later, will have his turn. The person has decided, perhaps beforehand, that this is the time when he is secure enough to claim help for himself. The group listens and begins to respond, if the member is genuinely asking for help: that is, if he shares what emotionally he struggles with. This emotionally charged feeling, need, or problem becomes the theme. Members begin to identify and share similarity of their feelings. Others come in to diagnose or make qualifications, and the group moves to the level of interaction. Eventually, group tension diminishes. One person may continue to talk, but soon he notes lack of group response; he too may become silent. The group becomes tense again and waits for a new direction to emerge.

The group leader may need to help the initiator get through to emotionally conflictual feelings, if the group does not get behind the language of words to the troubled person. Clarifying questions and responses serve this purpose. Also, the counselor senses when the theme has been exhausted. Interpretations at this point summarize and consolidate the group's experience, whereas interpretations made at the height of group interaction are not heard.

Developmental Phases of Group Life

Like an individual, a group goes through several developmental stages. These phases chart movement from inception to becoming a mature, fully functional group. There are at least five of these levels:

1. Getting started: anticipatory anxiety, leader dependency, and goal orientation.
2. Sharing information: getting acquainted and testing others.
3. Sharing feelings: experiencing acceptance and trust.
4. Confrontation and emotional encounter: emotionally corrective events.
5. Member autonomy and group interdependence: selfhood-in-community.

Getting Started. This first stage was discussed in Chapter 6; however, clarification and identification of purpose or goal was treated as a part of structure. Obviously, developmental stages are not marked off with clearly defined boundaries; they interpenetrate one another. Furthermore, the analogy of group development compared with that of an individual breaks down. A group is composed of adults with skills already actualized in various degrees. Some members have much less difficulty "getting started." They jump quickly to phase two or three. Groups vary; some will linger for several weeks in phase one or two. Another group may move quickly to phase three, if members have been intimately acquainted previously. Individuals in the group can be located within the several levels; this is particularly true when new members come into a group that is well along its way.

Sharing Information. As in individual counseling, the counselee's fear of rejection is paramount in early sessions. Usually he begins at the less threatening level and shares what he feels will be more acceptable. He presents himself in a favorable light, and several sessions may be necessary before he moves to reveal personal weaknesses and limitations. These areas of vulnerability to self-esteem are cautiously approached. Members carefully test each other to make sure it is relatively safe before making personal, "incriminating" disclosures. Information shared often is evidence that indicts one's spouse, parents, boss, or another convenient scapegoat. This protective device is as old as the human race. "The man said, 'The woman whom thou gavest to be with me, she gave me fruit of the tree and I ate'" (Genesis 3:12 RSV).

Such sharing is a attempt to test out the group, to win sympathy and understanding for personal suffering and hurt, and to bring others into one's world as the informant perceives it. Other members raise questions because they, too, are in process of reliving their situation through the informant. They identify similarities and differences in their individual situations.

Bach labels this the level of "advising and socializing."[2] Participants derive real values out of socializing their complaints. It is necessary to deal first with that which is external to oneself before moving to the internal agenda.

During this time, members engage in considerable "counseling" of one another, or giving of advice. Members diagnose what is wrong in another's life situation and what corrective steps should be taken, or they engage in the power of positive thinking, seeking to underplay the seriousness of difficulty and to admonish the informant to look on the brighter side. Those who take helper roles avoid coming to terms with their own problems. They occupy positions of strength by focusing on the needs and weaknesses of another. In this posture, they do not make themselves vulnerable. Bach likens this phase to a "peer court," with prosecuting and defending attorneys and listening jurors. Eventually the "defendant" comes to his own defense. He resists being singled out for "trial." His resistance takes a strong

2 *Op. cit.*, p. 94.

or weak form. He may become hostile, turn and attack! Or he (more often she) begins to cry. At this point, advisers reverse roles and become empathetic and supportive. Guilty feelings enter into the role switch; guilty feelings also motivate confession of faults and weaknesses.

While the peer court is in session, the counselor is limited to pointing out what the group is doing. His observation may not be heard. When the group declares the trial invalid, it is in position to examine what has happened. The accused also emerges with new strength to take his place among his peers.

Sharing Feelings. The third major shift in group direction comes as participants move from the sharing of ideas to the sharing of feelings. This does not mean that feelings have not been expressed at all previously; feelings have been in evidence in complaints about others. Ideas have been the predominant vehicles of communication, however.

Now participants have become acquainted and experience growing acceptance and trust. The expression of feeling grows. A member is secure enough to move to the center of the circle which is himself. He expresses how he feels about himself and within himself.

Participants sense that they are on "holy ground" as one of them lifts the veil that separates the inner man from the external world. Members are quiet, speak softly, and pay rapt attention. At the same time, the counselor is aware that each participates deeply in his own world of feeling as well as that of the speaker. They speak comforting words born of empathy and of identification with an experience common to many in the group. This sharing by one opens up the way for others to report similar feelings and experiences.

What happens at this level is the *gift of acceptance* for the unacceptable. A person shares that which is most unacceptable in his experience. This may be feelings of unattractiveness, lack of self-worth, inferiority, sexual inadequacy; fears of homosexuality, insanity, infanticide; guilty over incapacity to love, or a premarital pregnancy. Responses communicate: "You are accepted. Having shared this, you have only revealed to us how human you are. We feel comfortable with you because you have let us know you. And in knowing you, you have helped us to know ourselves better. To tell the truth, we are very much like you."

The acceptance given to a member is also acceptance given to oneself. It also provides incentive for each member to take his turn in inviting others into confidence. Thus, for several sessions, members share material that is deeply emotionally laden. The atmosphere of the group is one of trust and acceptance.

Each session does not begin at this level. Members still have to warm up and socialize. They get off in intellectual discussions. The counselor's task is to remind them what they are doing. He frequently recalls the group to its task: "I wonder if we are not spending our time intellectualizing, theologizing, and advising one another. Does this mean we are avoiding getting down to what really bothers us?" Eventually, a member (or members) become sensitive to this leadership task and group goal. He interrupts conversations and interprets group resistance.

Confrontation and Encounter. In the confessional and catharsis phase of ventilating and sharing unacceptable feelings, members gain emotional strength and courage. Energy that has been previously used to conceal and defend oneself from knowledge of others and from oneself is liberated for interpersonal investment. Also, each has gained a measure of security; he has been affirmed as a person who is liked and accepted. The group has given each person position and status; the group has become a group and each member feels a worthful and valid part of it.

Kurt Lewin discovered that the certainty of a member depends upon his feeling sure of the "ground" upon which he stands. The firmness of his actions and the clearness of decisions, according to Lewin[3] and Murray,[4] depend largely upon this ground—that of the group's acceptance and affirmation. This brings with it a new freedom. Having become a part, one has new freedom and has courage to operate with more autonomy.

Individual differences begin to surface. The previous phase is more one of agreement and affirmation. Now agreement in subgroups continues but disagreement and encounter between subgroups become

[3] Kurt Lewin, *Resolving Social Conflicts: Selected Papers on Group Dynamics,* edited by G. W. Lewin (New York: Harper, 1948), p. 145.

[4] I am indebted to Carl C. Murray, a pastoral intern at the Institute of Religion, Texas Medical Center, Houston, Texas, for the insight in his unpublished research paper "The Relevance of Kurt Lewin's Concept of the Group to Paul's Understanding of the Nature of the Church, As Expressed in His Metaphor of the Body of Christ." Fall, 1962.

the rule. We have moved to the phase of confrontation and encounter.

The phase of agreement and confirmation provides emotionally corrective experience in the area of a person's feelings and attitudes toward himself. The stage of confrontation and encounter makes available emotionally corrective experience in the area of relationship and behavior that involves others. At this level, one gets a reading and evaluation as to how his behavior affects his contemporaries in and outside the group.

To illustrate:

Felix: When Martha and the children get on the bus, they take seats by themselves. The whole cotton picking bunch don't open their mouths at all. And me with my big mouth, I like to get on the bus, "Hi, bus driver! How're you doing? This bus going by the zoo? We got a whole pack of monkeys here." [Meaning his family]

Tina: (With agitation) But you may embarrass them.

Felix: (Loudly) I do embarrass the hell out of them. Yeah. (Several people trying to talk) But with me, see, I think this is fine. (Others trying to break in) The other night I was on the bus, way in the back minding my own business and Mabel [a group member] gets on. First thing I can do is (emits two shrill whistles; group laughs) whistle at her three or four times. (Group talks in background, still trying to get through)

Tina: You can't expect a very pleasant reaction from . . .

Felix: (Continuing) Hi Mabel! M-a-bel! She doesn't pay any attention to me!

Tina: I don't blame her.

Felix: You don't? Aha. (Several still trying to talk, but group breaks forth in raucous laughter) Well, nobody got hurt!

Mabel: (After laughter subsides) This is very clear in my mind. It just happened yesterday. I'd like to say something . . . it occurs to me, I never had an opportunity to say it to anyone before, *I was very much embarrassed.* I realized in a way it was funny because you and I are such extremes. I'm so "shoved down" and you are "Wow" (throws hands upward and outward, indicating explosive); (Mabel tells this episode over and traces hurt and embarrassment to earlier experiences) When a person is unattractive and a whistle like this comes and people look, there is such a discrepancy between what they expect to see and what they do see. Then it makes the contrast that much more vivid. And I *shrink* from this . . . in past experience when someone whistled and I looked, someone would say, "I don't mean you, I mean that girl over there." This *hurts*. I was *scared* to death you would see me get off.

Felix:　　I saw you get off.

Mabel:　　I almost panicked for fear you would holler something else.

Felix:　　(Tells of his conversation with another on the bus in which he speaks of Mabel as a good friend) (To Mabel) I think it was your own inhibitions that caused you to become hurt. (Relates how another friend is able to laugh off his antics)

Tina:　　I feel the way Mabel does and also, while Mabel was talking, I was thinking, that "probably one of the reasons why your relationship with Martha is not any better, you can't just knock someone around and expect to have a relationship. I think you're going to have to start and really win her over, if you want a relationship . . . I don't think you can treat women this way and (Firmly) I don't think you should whistle at Mabel on the bus.

Felix:　　(Somewhat subdued) O.K., thank you. (Loudly again) I can yell at her, not whistle at her, huh?

Tina:　　(More firmly) No, you don't do that either (Silence).

Felix:　　O.K.

Tina:　　I've wanted to say this for a long time.

Felix:　　(Wrinkling his brow and pursing his lips) I can accept your thought, but whether I'm going to react the way you want me to react, I can't promise you. (Silence) Because it would not be me if I could not express myself.

Tina:　　(Tone and volume rising) But you express yourself to the detriment of other people! This is . . . kind of primitive of you . . .

Felix:　　(Interrupting) What you're doing, you're being prudish . . . now.

Tina: It isn't being prudish at all.

Felix: Huh?

Tina: I don't know any wife who likes that kind of treatment. (Silence)

Felix: I guess you're right.

Tina: I didn't expect that reaction. (Group laughs again)

The theories of Kurt Lewin contribute significantly to understanding of forces in a group that effect change in its members. The values, goals, and behavior of a person, he maintains, are deeply influenced by the social values, standards, and goals of groups to which he belongs or wishes to belong. The standards that determine behavior of an individual are therefore not primarily those of the individual but those of his most important social groups. Groups have decisive influence because of the need of each to belong, to be on the inside of the group. For this reason, a person undergoes change easier in a group than when counseled privately.

In the encounter quoted above, Felix relates an event in which he acts out his need to express himself. The group of which he is a member adheres to a committed goal—that of interpersonal values, learning to relate to others with regard for their feelings, values, and strivings as well as one's own. The behavior of Felix violated the group standard; as a result, the group disciplined him. The power of the group at this point far exceeds the influence of a single therapist. Out of this encounter, Felix begins to be sensitized to the values of the group and at the same time is called to relate to others within and outside the group on the basis of genuine regard for the others' rights and feelings.

One may argue that Felix complies or submits while in counseling but that once out of the sphere of influence of the counseling group, his leopard spots remain. But for Felix this will not be so. He is deeply committed to the group; it is very meaningful to him, and he is one of its helpful members. When he formally leaves, he takes the group with him. Experiences in depth groups are internalized as are its members; for years after formal leave-taking, in crucial and crisis experiences, Felix will remember the above encounter and other cardinal events. He will recall what Mabel told him and what Tina said. Like departed saints, "Being dead, yet they live and speak." When members belong to the same church fellowship, their postgroup contacts serve to call all things to remembrance.

All change is not immediate in group counseling. Seeds planted continue to bear fruit. The Holy Spirit continues His ministry. During the time when one is in a group, he is often unaware of changes in feelings, attitudes, and modes of relating. Change becomes more apparent months after, when one gains the perspective of distance. The meaningful values of the group continue as "leaven in the loaf."

Member Autonomy and Group Interdependence. The final stage is that in which a member experiences his own separate identity or individuality. As one person recently affirmed, "I am beginning to feel my own separateness, to feel my own feelings, and think my own thoughts. I feel more sure about making decisions, even though I may make mistakes." One has the capacity to take a stand against others, to engage in spontaneous free communication of ideas and feeling, to make decisions and follow through. He is in touch with himself. He has "enlarged the tent" of his own self-awareness, reclaimed and accepted hidden treasures within himself, and become more self-affirmative and decisive. He experiences himself as a Self.

His individuality, however, does not isolate him from the group. He belongs and is a participant, as well as a part. He need not defend himself against the group, as a way of preserving his identity and separateness. Neither does his selfhood become submerged in the group and lost as the price of belonging. *He experiences authentic selfhood-in-community.*

This is the developmental destiny of each person. This is one's ultimate personal and spiritual destiny, when the ground of selfhood and community is God, who is recognized and worshiped. As such, authentic selfhood-in-community is the goal toward which each member and the group as a whole strive.

Andras Angyal[5] interprets the polar nature of personality described above. He identifies three basic trends in polar tension with each other: the heteronomous, the autonomous, and the homonomous trends. The first, heteronomy, points to the early dependency and being controlled or determined by the external world of persons and things. The second, autonomy, describes the tension within to become free and independent. Finally, homonomy represents the need

[5] Andras Angyal, *Foundations for a Science of Personality* (New York: The Commonwealth Fund, 1941).

to belong to and be participant in a community that is larger than oneself—the move to interdependence. When one trend predominates and is not balanced by other needs, one is a sick or crippled self.

Søren Kierkegaard[6] many years ago delineated three forms of sick selves—the self unaware that it is a self; the self that wills to be a self defiantly; and the self, conscious of being a self but unable to will to be a self. A parallelism exists here between Kierkegaard's formula and that of Angyal. The mentally healthy person is one in whom those three needs are held in homeostasis or balanced tension.

Martin Buber has another way of perceiving this goal of authentic selfhood-in-community. He lifts up a twofold principle of movement in man: (1) "The primal setting of distance"; and (2) "entering into relation."[7] The capacity to distance himself or to be transcendent, and the capacity to enter into relation, distinguish man from the rest of nature. Distance is a prerequisite for entering relationships. Real relationships are characterized by dialogue—the acceptance of the "otherness" of the other person and being fully present to listen and respond to his address. To be responsible and fully human is to live the life of dialogue. Even one's potentialities are not known and experienced except as they are called forth as one meets the demands in dialogic communication and encounter. " 'All real living is meeting.' Individuation is not the goal but only the indispensable way to the goal."[8]

The relation between man and man is not only an I-Thou or one-to-one relationship; it is also the "We of Community":

> As the "primitive Thou" precedes the consciousness of individual separateness, whereas the "essential Thou" follows and grows out of this consciousness, so the "primitive We" precedes true individuality and independence, whereas the "essential We" only comes about when independent people have come together in essential relation and directness. The essential We includes the Thou po-

[6] Søren Kierkegaard, The Sickness Unto Death (Princeton: Princeton University Press, 1946).

[7] Maurice Friedman, "Dialogue and the 'Essential We.' The Basic Values in the Philosophy of Martin Buber." Group Psychotherapy and Group Function, edited by Max Rosenbaum and Milton Berger (New York: Basic Books, Inc., 1963).

[8] Ibid., p. 607.

tentially, for "only men who are capable of truly saying *Thou* to one another can truly say *We* with one another." This We is not of secondary or merely instrumental importance; it is basic to existence, and as such it is a prime source of value.[9]

For this reason, true guilt is the failure to respond to the legitimate claims and address of one's world:

> Existential guilt is the corollary of the answerability and responsibility of the self in the concrete dialogical situation. It is failure to respond and, by the same token, failure to authenticate one's existence.[10]

Martin Buber, among others, again helps us to perceive the cogent value of counseling groups as a medium through which individuals become more fully human.

Transactions Within and Between Subgroups

We have hitherto looked at processes within the group as a whole. We turn now to *part processes,* one of which is that of subgrouping. As we have seen, considerable pressure is present for members to change attitudinal values and behavior in line with group standards. Subgroups develop as a form of resistance to group pressure, to provide pockets of refuge from threat, as a means of exerting power and influence, and as an expression of attraction between the sexes. Bach[11] identifies four psychological functions of subgroups:

Confluence. On occasion, one or more members overidentify or merge their personality with the operations of a stronger member. They gear their behavior and responses to comply or agree with the expectations and mode of relating of the other. In other words, a subgroup based on confluence consists of persons flowing together, with a stronger pivotal member, like two merging streams. This operation provides a sense of security, belonging, strength, and base from which to communicate in the total group.

Release Associations. Other subgroups form on the basis of friendship, particularly outside the group. Common interest, tele-

9 *Ibid.,* p. 610.
10 *Ibid.,* p. 611.
11 *Op. cit.,* p. 394.

phone conversations, and social events provide a ground for talking about feelings, problems, and needs that are more easily introduced at the subgroup level in extra-group communication.

Coalitions. Subgroups also form on the basis of power motives. Such subgroups seek to exert influence and sometimes control of nonmembers (of the subgroup). For example, a man brought a list of Scripture verses selected from Proverbs that describe the evils of seductive and nagging women. He solicited the support of two male members and they attempted to subordinate the women in the group. The women were joined by one male member and the "battle of the sexes" was on, with each group seeking to incriminate the other.

Pairing. A fourth subgroup formation stems from attraction between the sexes. Single people with difficulty in relating to the other sex venture forth toward one another in the security of the group. In nonchurch groups, the acting out of neurotic needs in group sessions and frank discussion of sexual attraction to a group member are frequent topics. Incidences of actual sexual liaisons between group members are very low. In church groups, although sexual pairing takes place, members are less open to discuss it; more reserve exists. Members discuss more their fear of extramarital sexual involvement. The question of marriage between group members is discussed in the final chapter.

Positive Value of Subgroups. Subgroups have a constructive function. They serve as a ground for intense catharsis, acting out, encounter, and confrontation. Diversity of opinion is essential for maintenance of group pressure and tension. Pressure to change increases with increasing difference of opinion—that is, if the group sustains cohesiveness.[12] Diversity of opinion also reduces the dependency of members on the total group. Each person sustains status, power, and individuality through subgrouping. Members of subgroups have very positive therapeutic effects on each other. The passive member may identify with the more aggressive member. Out of their teamed relationship, the passive member begins to emulate the more outgoing partner. Or, the wife without children and the mother whose children are adults find occasion to nurture those deprived of mother love. Confession made to subgroup mem-

[12] Stanley Schaeter, "Deviation, Rejection, and Communication." *Group Dynamics: Research and Theory.* Edited by Darwin Cartwright and Alvin Zander (Evanston: Row, Peterson & Co., 1953), p. 231.

bers in postgroup session also is prelude to sharing in the total group. Old subgroups give way to new ones; the older ones have served their purpose. When the need for a certain one no longer exists, new kinds of alliances are formed with other members. Shifts and changes represent movement and growth. The emotional child in the adult gives way to more mature needs and relationships.

Therapeutic subgrouping, however, never strays far from the cohesive purpose and goal of the group as a whole. If it does, it becomes a splinter-group formation, representing those who are not really committed to the therapeutic task. Drop-outs can be in part attributed to poor motivation for growth and change.

Subgroups and Member Problems. In early phases of group life, subgroups are used as a means of neurotic defense and for acting out repressed needs and wishes. Bach calls these "neurotic set-up operations" and lists five patterns of neurotic relationships that are acted out in subgroups:

1. *Projections,* or attributing motives, problems, or ideas to another which are really in oneself. One member, for example, frequently charged women in the group with what were obviously his own problems.
2. *Externalizations,* or empathetically sensing and talking about the problems of another but failing to recognize the same difficulty in one's self.
3. *Distortions,* believing other people have ideas or feelings or way of relating toward oneself which they do not have.
4. *Acted-Out Transferences,* that is, acting toward group members as if they were like significant persons in the early family, such as mother, brother, father, friend, etc.
5. *Acted-Out Countertransferences,* or when another member responds in a complementary way and acts upon the image or role which another member has attributed to him.[13]

Group members are able to diagnose and interpret when a member or subgroup member distorts reality. The group as a whole is strongly oriented to reality and resists distortions. The group leader helps examine in depth these self-protective devices that either isolate one from true relation or that exploit another to fulfill repressed instinctual or emotional needs.

[13] *Op. cit.,* p. 399.

Individual Movement
in Self-Disclosure and Self-Discovery

Action and movement go on not only in the group as a whole and in subgroups but also within each member. Nathan Ackerman[14] defines two basic concepts for understanding an individual in a group. These are self-identity and role behavior. Identity refers to the conscious, structured, historical experience that a person identifies as himself. This would include values, needs, goals, and strivings. Role behavior is the way a person integrates his identity into a group. Group counseling operates at both levels. On one hand, an individual improves his role behavior in interpersonal situations. On the other, he becomes more acquainted with himself and undergoes changes in the way he views and feels toward himself. This happens as one explores and shares various levels and dimensions of his self-experience. Several progressive levels can be identified:

1. *Identifying Self in the Presenting Problem:* How one perceives and feels about the conflict situation is told. A person talks primarily about the problems of his spouse or significant other, such as a parent. Following this, a group helps an individual look at his own contribution to the difficulty.

2. *Identifying Self Through the Personal History:* This next step looks for causes and understanding of who one is and how he came to be this way. Each goes back to share aspects of personal and social history. Considerable feeling and blame is attributed to parents, siblings, and others. Ventilation serves to effect emancipation from dependent, ambivalent, or hostile feelings that chain one to his past and/or present.

3. *Identifying Self in Feelings About Oneself:* At this phase, the individual ceases to project blame on others and begins to "look to himself." He assumes responsibility for his own nature and destiny. He takes upon himself responsibility for his past, present, and future. He works through feelings, fears, and hurts that have called defensive, isolating, manipulative tactics into interpersonal operations.

4. *Synthesis: A More Unified, Accepting, and Affirming Self:*

[14] *The Psychodynamics of Family Life: Diagnosis and Treatment of Family Relationships* (New York: Basic Books, Inc., 1958).

Here the person has assimilated and integrated into his self-system the relationship of past, present, and anticipated future experiences.

Group and Member Movement
in Relation to the Group Counselor

A final part process involves the relationships between the group, the individual members, and the counselor. We have already described phases of group resistance when a counselor no longer meets dependency needs and members accept responsibility for each other. At a later stage, the counselor has the over-all respect and trust. Members understand and accept his function of facilitating the group process, but no longer look to him to solve their problems. Positive feelings of appreciation are expressed on occasions. In the words of several, "We want to thank you for your help. There are times when we would have become lost in our discussion had you not been here to help us see what we were dealing with and its relevance for our lives." Here the counselor's "expert" role is recognized and affirmed. Or, as a member who had invited her group to a luncheon said, "I don't think I want to do that again. Without you being present, I became so angry that I was literally astonished at myself."

The counselor is never a member in the same sense that others in the group are. He does not share in postgroup meetings and social affairs. These are occasions when members have a freedom to engage in conversation that may at first be withheld from the formally structured sessions. Furthermore, the counselor does not share his own problems at length with the group, nor do they expect him to.

Individual members continue to *act out* authority problems in relation to the counselor. Some compete with him for leadership. Some compete with each other for a privileged relationship with him. Ambivalent feelings—at times positive appreciation and, at others, resentment and anger—show through. Silences, noncooperativeness, and withdrawal from participation express passive rebellion and defiance and yet appeal for counselor love, attention, and concern. Open defiance and hostility break through toward the counselor at times.

These reactions are more frequent and intense when counselors are very active and assume a definite authority role. When the counselor is group-oriented, these reactions are more frequently directed at group members who play out authority and leader roles.

Again, members pick up and discuss these operations. At times, the counselor calls upon the group to explore these events, or he may engage a particular member first in dialogue and then call the group to report observations and feelings.

Dynamics in Group Counseling

Dynamics are those forces at work in the field situation of a group; it is these forces that account for therapeutic benefits. Raymond J. Corsini[15] with Rosenberg, surveyed 300 articles in the literature on group psychotherapy and found authors listing 166 different "mechanisms" or dynamisms. They break these down into three major categories under which significant dynamisms are subsumed.

Emotional Factors. A group offers three basic emotional gifts: *Acceptance* is summed up in words like "friendly environment, espirit de corps, communal feeling, togetherness, supportive relations, identification with others, loss of isolation, etc." *Altruism* refers to the way each gains "the sense of being important in the lives of others, being a therapist for one another such as giving advice, support, and love." *Transference* is "the cement that makes a group. . . . It is the identification with each other through the common attachment to the leader." All three of these are part of what it means to give and receive love.

Intellectual Factors. *Spectator therapy* is experiencing vicariously in, through, and with experiences of others. Nonverbal members are helped by listening to and observing other participants. One is able to see himself objectified in the experience of other members. *Universalization* is the dynamic at work when a person suddenly finds he is not the only person with a problem or that problems of others are very similar to one's own. One member at first had difficulty believing that two others "needed to be in a group." She had always considered them "strong and effective" and herself weak and inefficient. It is a relief to join the human race and not feel so different. *Intellectualization* gives one an opportunity to rethink or re-evaluate concepts. At times, one acquires information previously unknown.

[15] *Methods of Group Psychotherapy* (New York: McGraw-Hill Book Co., 1957), pp. 38–48.

On other occasions, what he has known all the time comes alive in a new and meaningful way.

Action Factors. *Reality testing* "lies at the heart" of group counseling. Therapeutic groups provide a field for social relationships in which a person can test his defenses ". . . relive old family conflicts, live out ego frustrations, and find outlets for aggression." *Ventilation* provides release of suppressed and repressed emotions, needs, and drives. Finally, beneficial results accrue from *interaction*. If a group meets seriously for therapy and engages in maximal relationship, therapy takes place, regardless of what is discussed or what methods are used. Thus Corsini reduces dynamic factors to a basic minimum of nine items. He also suggests that methods of therapy can be classified according to whether the counselor gives prior attention to emotional, intellectual, or actional factors operative in a group.

CHAPTER EIGHT

TECHNIQUES Of GROUP COUNSELING

Techniques are special methods or means through which a pastoral counselor makes himself available to a group. Techniques are not to be conceived as ways by which he imposes his own way or wisdom. Expertness as a leader manifests itself as the leader's initiative and action express who he is and as these are consistent with his attitudes and belief that the Holy Spirit can be trusted to perform His work. Furthermore, counselor interventions are consistent with the leader's basic trust in a group's ability to assume responsibility for the healing of its members. His leadership is suggestive rather than didactic or persuasive. Techniques become tactics by which the work of the group is facilitated and deepened.

Major Functions of the Counselor

The counselor has three primary tasks. These are *procedural, catalytic,* and *interpretative functions.*[1]

Procedural Functions. Many of the procedural tasks were discussed in Chapter 6 in connection with ordering the life of a group. After the leader-dependency phase, the counselor may employ "programmic" procedures that enable a group to move more quickly to its work or that enable members to review their progress. Through procedural functions, the counselor fulfills his "kingly" or administrative role as minister to the group. Programmic procedures also serve as catalysts of group process. Several of these will merit special attention later.

Catalytic Functions. The counselor's own *feelings,* as well as his verbal participation and nonverbal gestures, have a catalytic effect on the group. The counselor is not feelingly detached and remote

[1] George R. Bach, *Intensive Group Psychotherapy* (New York: Ronald Press Co., 1954), p. 47.

from the group. He is emotionally as well as intellectually and actionally present. At times he responds with understanding that communicates tenderness, warmth, and support. He also interprets hostile and angry communications on occasion by emotionally experiencing with the hurt, angry, hostile feelings of members. He is "made like his brethren in every respect" that he may be a faithful priest (Hebrews 2:17). He can "rejoice with those who rejoice, weep with those who weep" (Romans 12:15). He will experience his own suffering and joy as well as that of others. He is identified as a human being with others in the sin and suffering that are our common experience and in the common need for continuing healing and growth.

Counselor participation is often described as though the counselor belonged to the *neuter* gender. This may be an attempt to avoid "countertransferences" in which the counselor becomes victim and/or culprit by responding to neurotic needs, expectations, and interpersonal operations in a complementary or resistive fashion. Countertransferences are nontherapeutic and are to be avoided when possible. When they do occur, they can be analyzed as part of the group's experience.

The counselor can look at manifestations of his own sin, sickness, and incompleteness when these show up in a group. As James Baldwin says:

> The questions which one asks oneself begin, at last, to illumine the world and become one's key to the experience of others. One can only face in others what one can face in oneself. On this confrontation depends the measure of our wisdom and compassion.[2]

The group leader usually will discuss his own personal problems and his problems of leadership outside the group with another who ministers to him—his wife, another counselor, or pastor.

The counselor's feelings become catalytic and therapeutic when his nonverbal as well as verbal communications indicate understanding and appreciation of what participants experience. Such responses convey "being" with the other, communicate acceptance, and facilitate further ventilation of feelings. Counselor responses are also catalytic when he engages in confrontation and encounter and when

[2] James Baldwin, *Nobody Knows My Name* (New York: Dell Publishing Co., Inc., 1961), p. 13.

he calls upon a member to reconsider, examine, and explore aspects of behavior highlighted by an encounter.

Although the counselor should be emotionally present in the group, again we remind the reader that the stance, role, and function of the pastoral group counselor are different from those of the counselees. The counselor is a participant observer. He does not become overidentified and participate emotionally at the same depth and intensity that the parishioner does. He maintains a certain distance, detachment, and objectivity along with his participant involvement. Successful counseling depends upon the maintenance of the tension of the detachment-participation polarity. It also depends upon the counselor's ability to move back and forth on this polar continuum and on the appropriate timing of his responses, which are more or less emotionally participative in nature or more or less emotionally detached. Buber's interpreter, Maurice Friedman, makes explicit that "healing through meeting" is a one-sided inclusion:

> In friendship and love, "inclusion," or experiencing the other side, is mutual. In the helping relationships, however, it is necessarily one-sided. The patient cannot equally well experience the relationship from the side of the therapist or the pupil from the side of the teacher without destroying or fundamentally altering the relationship. This does not mean that the therapist, for example, is reduced to treating his patient as an object, an It. The one-sided inclusion of therapy is still an "I-Thou" relation founded on mutuality, trust, and partnership in a common situation and it is only in this relation that real therapy can take place. If "all real living is meeting, all true healing takes place through meeting . . . the regeneration of an atrophied personal center . . . can only . . . be attained in the person-to-person attitude of a partner, not by the consideration and examination of an object." *But a common situation does not mean one which each enters from the same or even similar position. In psychotherapy the difference in position is not only that of personal stance, but of role and function, a difference determined by the very difference of purpose which led each to enter the relationship* [italics mine]. If the goal is a common one—the healing of the patient—the relationship to that goal differs radically as between therapist and patient, and healing that takes place depends as much upon the recognition of that difference as upon the mutuality of meeting and trust.[3]

[3] Maurice Friedman, "Dialogue and the 'Essential We,' the Basis of Values in the Philosophy of Martin Buber," *Group Psychotherapy and Group Function, op. cit.,* p. 609.

Interpretative Functions. The task of interpretation is a third major function of the pastoral group counselor. "Interpretative communications have teaching as their objective. They are utilized primarily to help the person become aware of his previous and present forms of interpersonal relatedness."[4] Interpretations bring unknown and unrelated aspects of experience into focus and give insight into experience that previously was without shape or meaning. Awareness and understanding of the source and nature of personal difficulty help one in problem solving. Occasionally, after an interpretation, a member will ask, "Now that I partly understand the cause of my trouble, what can I do about it?" The counselor may reply, "Perhaps now you can see your situation in a new light and perspective. This does not change your situation, but it does change your understanding. On the basis of this new awareness, other possibilities of viewing and acting are opened to you." Interpretations are made from four categories of experience: (1) feelings within and about oneself; (2) relationships within the family; (3) relationships within the group; and (4) religious questions or concerns. Themes of the group (see Chapter 7) shift back and forth among these areas. Most interpretative work relates to dynamics of behavior captured and communicated in group themes.

In a compilation of the themes of five counseling groups in a total of 50 recorded sessions, there were a total of 72 topics. These were further classified as follows with topics that recurred several times indicated:

1. *Feelings regarding oneself* (28); need for self-acceptance, search for identity, sense and/or fear of isolation, relational insensitivity, authority problems.

2. *Marital problems* (18); need of love from spouse, need of love from parents, parental domination and inability to give love, marital roles and introjected parental images, problems in nurture vs. discipline of children.

3. *Group relationships* (20); fear of hurt and difficulty in trusting others, difficulty in communicating feelings, group purpose and goal, fear of self-revelation, resistance to psychological tests, member termination, member monopolist, appreciation for value of group.

4 Joseph W. Knowles, "The Mental Hospital Chaplain as a Counselor with Schizophrenic Persons." Unpublished doctoral dissertation, Southern Baptist Theological Seminary, Louisville, Kentucky, January, 1954.

4. *Religious concerns* (5); prayer, defensive and creative.

Several topics are duplicated in more than one group or repeated in the same group to increase the total number to 107 topics. These themes indicate not only what the groups discussed, but problems either they or the counselor interpreted as to genesis, dynamics, and/or meaning.

Principles of interpretation answer the questions of what, when, and how to interpret. Interpretation of conflictual feelings and their origin takes precedence over content or ideas. Timing is also important. On the whole, the counselor should have a positive relationship to the group, a relationship in which he is trusted and accepted before becoming interpretative. A member should have worked through an experience sufficiently to have some understanding of it. Interpretation, furthermore, depends on the security and strength within the member or group. Material that will be excessively threatening is not interpreted until one can really "hear" and appropriate it. Finally, interpretations should be brief, direct, clear, and one-sided. Fromm-Reichmann notes that "questioning in terms of 'either/or' tends to be confusing and therefore anxiety-producing. . . ."[5]

Programmic Methods

Programmic procedures serve several purposes. They may be used to get a group started, to secure additional information, to involve a member or a group with feeling experience, to clarify group goal and process, to test participants' understanding of group purpose, or to investigate and analyze group processes. Programmic procedures may be initiated *spontaneously* by a member or *suggested* by the counselor. For example, a member may wonder how others in the group experience him and ask for their opinion. In this instance, the member spontaneously employs one of the procedures discussed below.

Selection of a Theme and Presenter. Normally the group evolves its own theme or themes. Conversation begins at a social level until a member introduces a significant topic. Following the group phase of leader dependency, however, the counselor may take more initiative without the danger of fostering group dependency on him.

---

[5] Gustav Bychowski and J. Louise Despert, editors, *Specialized Techniques in Psychotherapy* (New York: Basic Books, Inc., 1952), p. 168.

On occasion, a group may be a slow starter. The counselor may lead in exploring why the group has difficulty becoming airborne. In another procedure, the counselor asks each participant to tell what problem he would like to discuss, and each names a topic or passes. When all members have stated their preferences, a vote is taken on the topic of most interest to the group as a whole. The person naming the topic is asked to share his concerns that focus around it. The group thus moves rapidly to a consensus as to a theme and presenter.

Role Playing. Role playing is a dramatic technique in which two or more members act out a scene or episode they have just discussed. This is a marvelous method for assisting members to move from a descriptive, intellectualizing posture to one of experiencing feelings associated with an event or problem. Role playing enables members to relive a situation as it is dramatized. Also, a dramatic production depicts a situation more accurately than a mere description. To illustrate, John monologued in a detached manner the problem of enforcing discipline of a teen-age daughter. The daughter would not permit him to come into her room. When he tried, she became defiant and abusive. He did not know how to cope with such behavior, particularly since his wife refused to support him, he said, and resisted any disciplinary action on his part. Members of the group tried to involve themselves with John but could not draw him out of his detachment, partly signaled by his inability to look at others while he talked. The counselor suggested a role play. John was invited to play the part of the daughter, to which he readily assented, and Ellen was invited to act out John's part. The role play emotionally involved both John and the group to a significant degree. A role play production has several steps:

1. Defining the problem
2. Casting characters
3. Briefing and warming up
4. The role play
5. Analysis and discussion

Usually, a member has defined the problem and given considerable background information before a role play is suggested. Members are invited to assume a role rather than volunteer or be assigned. The counselor can select those who can play a certain role well or those who can profit from acting out a role that is different from their habitual mode of behavior, thus allowing a member to experience himself in a new way and to develop new skills. In the above role play, John played the daughter because he could best represent her to the group and he needed to ventilate his own feelings via the role of a defiant child. Ellen could play the parent role well because it was consistent with her own family role.

Briefing and warm-up is a phase in which characters are asked if they desire additional information. The counselor may question each to ascertain whether they know what part they are playing and what feelings and actions the part calls for. During the role play itself, the counselor may be seated or may stand to one side in the role of drama director. Occasionally, he may coach players. Following the scene, the group is invited to discuss their experience during the role play and to give their reactions to it. At times, a role play does not "come off," and participants can talk about their difficulty in playing the part. Alan F. Klein gives a detailed guide on role playing that counselors will find instructive.[6]

The Hot Seat. A third programmic method turns gossip into a therapeutic tool. Few people have the privilege of overhearing others "talk behind their backs." To one's face, others may screen what they say and think about him or feel toward him, but in his absence their hidden feeling and thoughts may be communicated.

The *hot seat* is a chair in a corner facing the wall. A member elects to go into the corner. Usually he requests this procedure, although at times the counselor may recommend it. The counselor each time instructs the group on the procedure and comments that "to hear what others actually feel and think is a rare privilege." The candidate, while facing the wall, is not permitted to speak; in fact, the counselor interprets as follows:

"Tom is not really in the room. Tom is not here. We are each to take a turn and say what we think about and feel toward Tom. In his absence, we will have the freedom to say to one another what we really feel and think. Evelyn, will you begin?"

The leader may ask specific questions or clarify the members' communication to help them verbalize. Once each has had an opportunity to contribute, the candidate is invited to join the group

[6] *Role Playing in Leadership Training and Group Problem-Solving* (New York: Association Press, 1956).

again. He has the privilege of sharing what his experience was in the corner and of addressing himself to particular members of the group. The hot seat is another means of involving members with one another and of enabling the candidate to see himself as others see him.

Going Around. The technique in selecting a theme and the hot seat procedure has employed the method of *going around.* This tactic is good for a number of purposes, such as to permit each to report on therapeutic progress or stalemate, to engage each in the interpretations of a group theme, or to enlist each in sharing his understanding of group goal, purpose, or process. Going around is one way to spread participation if two or three members talk excessively.

Dreams and Their Interpretation. Historically, dreams have been a means of revelation and insight. Through dreams, God has revealed His purposes to His servants. Freud refers to dreams as "the royal road to the unconscious." Dreams dramatize subjective reality— inner and interpersonal conflict and tension, repressed needs, and wish fulfillment. A member may report a dream and enlist others in search for its meaning. Or the counselor may ask if a participant has a recent dream to share.

No longer do most counselors trust a fixed code in which dream symbols have constant and universal meanings. The dream frequently is structured out of the stuff of recent experience. Often a series of dreams reveal a common theme that points to the nature of the dreamer's fear, struggle, or desire. The dreamer is the key to an understanding of the dream. As he and the group engage in associative thinking about the dream setting, fragments of the event and feelings associated with the dream, the counselor and the group help the person relate the dream to his personal history, problems, or experiences in the group. Calvin S. Hall's book on dream interpretation[7] will be of considerable assistance to the pastor.

Sharing Personal History. The counselor or a group member will ask a participant to set his problem in the context of his personal history. Sharing of personal history largely takes place early in group life. Members search for a "cause" for their dilemma. Blame is often shifted to parent and siblings. This sharing has therapeutic

[7] Calvin S. Hall, *The Meaning of Dreams* (New York: Harper & Bros., 1953).

value in that members gain strength and skill in verbalizing feelings and in finding a "logical" answer to puzzling and dark feelings or thoughts. Eventually, participants do not use historical data as a defense against shouldering responsibility for the past and becoming reconciled to it.

Psychological Test Results. When psychological tests are available, the counselor may use test results as a programmic procedure. He may use them in two ways. Some counselors keep all test results in their possession and share portions of each member's test at a time when the member is able to utilize these findings. This tactic is required by professional ethics when projective methods such as the Rohrschach or Thematic Apperception Tests or Intelligence Tests are administered by a professional psychologist. His report is confidential.

Tests available to prayer therapy groups may also be used in individual and group counseling. Test slips are written to be placed in the hands of group members. In short-term counseling, test slips may be distributed every other meeting. Test results should not be used until the group has developed autonomy and initiative, and has worked through early phases of group process.

The counselor's task is to lead group members to use test results as a way of discussing concrete personal experience. Discussion can remain on an intellectual level otherwise. The counselor may ask, "Can you give us a personal experience that illustrates the pattern to which the test points?" Testing thus serves as a springboard to personal self-confrontation.

Exploration of Social Relationships. Members are covenanted to report transactions with other members that transpire outside the group. Many groups get together for dinner or coffee and spend an hour or longer following each group session. Freedom of the social situation brings subgroup confluences, coalitions, and pairings into full bloom. Conversations also take place over the telephone or in visits to one another's homes. Periodically, the counselor introduces the theme of social relationship as a way to get members to examine and take stock of developments outside formal group counseling meetings.

Analysis of Subgrouping. Another tactic calls upon the group to note the patterns in which members team up with or against each other in group sessions. For instance, Tom was very resistive to his wife's insistent interpretation that his chronic lateness was a hostile act to her. Carol and Ellen, who previously supported each other, sided with Tom's wife. Their position also was undergirded by Alvin. John characteristically joined forces with Tom. Sarah and Naomi sustained their usual attempt to be conciliatory and belonged to both camps. Analysis of this subgroup formation brought out John's and Tom's covert hostility for their wives and Ellen's and Carol's overt hostility toward their husbands. The group also explored the insecurity and need Naomi and Sarah had for group approval. Finally, the group saw progress in Alvin's ability to recognize and accept his hostility, previously denied, as noted by his coalition with Ellen and Sarah.

Perceptions of Self and Others. Here a going-around procedure is used in two further ways. The counselor may ask each to share how he sees or experiences himself. Or a member may ask others how they see, understand, or experience him. The latter is a version of the hot seat, where one chooses to remain in face-to-face contact with the group.

Situation Analysis and Records

Powdermaker and Frank make use of situation analyses (written up in a consistent form) in order to study and evaluate positive and negative therapeutic effects of group events. They define a *situation* as "a series of events showing cause and effect relationship described with reference to the setting in which they occurred. Such a situation formed a kind of pattern, and some situations, we found, apparently formed similar patterns, which, when systematically compared, added to our understanding of treatment."[8]

The form of a situation analysis contains several elements. (1) The *setting* describes various aspects of the background significantly related to focal events of the group situation. (2) The *precipitating event* is a particular episode which triggers an event of group interaction. (3) The *event itself* is an occurrence "which was accompanied or immediately followed by a change in tension, behavior, or attitude." (4) Finally, the effects represent results growing out of the

[8] Florence B. Powdermaker and Jerome D. Frank, *Group Psychotherapy: Studies in Methodology of Research and Therapy* (Cambridge, Mass.: Harvard University Press, 1953), p. 23 ff.

interaction, including therapeutic progress of members. To illustrate, the following is an analysis of an initial meeting.

Dr. K's Group, Meeting 1—Situation Analysis A

SETTING

Doctor	Nonsupportive, passive, silent.
Group	Patients seemed to know that they should be discussing personal matters; afraid to reveal themselves to others; talked on impersonal topics. Tension rose.
Central patient	Hammond: dominating member, repeatedly tried to get focus of attention.
Situation preceding the rally	Group talked on impersonal topics.
Precipitating event	Doctor intervened: "Have you any idea of the trend of the discussion?" Tension rose sharply. Hammond, after trying in vain to question others, introduced rallying topic.
Event	Rally around topic: feelings about psychoanalysis and resistance to therapy.
Effects	Intimate discussion of illness. Relief of tension.

The above report shows how problems of a patient and a group are revealed in a situation analysis. Hammond seeks the spotlight and the group resists both the counselor and Hammond. This kind of study has one further advantage. It becomes a *simple method of record keeping* that charts the behavior of a group and ultimately each member in it. When several situation analyses are compared, progress or movement within the group and/or individual members can be seen.[9]

Multiple Counseling

Individual counseling becomes a helpful adjunct to group counseling for some participants. A few may require continuous individual counseling along with group counseling: the older adoles-

[9] *Ibid.*, Table 8, "Successful Rallying Topics."

cent who has not adequately symbolized his experience so that he is aware of it and can communicate it can make good use of concomitant individual sessions, for instance. This is true also of the parishioner who has experienced extreme trauma and deprivation. He may be unable at first to talk about deep personal wounds in the group. Self-preoccupation with intense and traumatic feeling hinders ability to be other-oriented. Communication of these concerns in private session releases one for involvement with and caring for other group members.

Sometimes members will ask for one private interview. The group may generate anxiety or tension in him which needs ventilation. He can safely express himself privately without fear of group disapproval or rejection. Others may hold grudges or have feelings of hostility or rivalry they fear to expose in the group. Individual counseling serves as a safety valve.

Several hindrances to healing can grow out of multiple counseling. Members may "drain off" feelings and experiences that should be shared in the group. Both the individual and the group are deprived if members report their problems only to the counselor in private. For this reason, some counselors employ individual counseling only for the purpose of enabling a participant to examine his group relationships. Private interviews also strengthen the bond to the counselor and afford access to him that other members do not have. This can create jealousy and hostility on the part of the nonprivileged and a sense of exclusive possession of the counselor on the part of the privately counseled. Those who need special attention may hesitate to ask for what they need, whereas those who have less need (but who can resist group pressure) may make demands. Discussion of these needs in the group creates a climate conducive for those who need special assistance to seek it.

Good counseling procedure forbids counselor disclosure in a group of confidences privately communicated. In the private interview, he may suggest the value of bringing confidences to the group. Or, in the group, he may ask the counselee leading questions that invite sharing. This depends on how well the person has mastered and assimilated unacceptable experience and upon his tolerance for group exposure at the moment. With a reasonably secure individual, the group counselor occasionally may invite contributions of privately discussed material that relates to a current group theme.

CHAPTER NINE

TECHNIQUES *Of* COUNSELING *In*

GROUP CRITICAL INCIDENTS

Methods of leadership have been of prime concern in most of the previous discussion. Critical problems arise, however, which require special attention. Any significant behavior that deviates from the group's committed purpose may produce a critical incident or event or moment when the progress of a member or the group hangs in the balance. It can become a creative moment of growth, new awareness, and entrance into a new realm of being, or it may signal a falling away or falling back that evokes the defenses of the "old man" (Ephesians 4:22).

To some extent, the fate of the group is linked with the fate of each member. Paul's statement is literally true: "If one member suffers, all suffer together; if one member is honored, all rejoice together" (I Corinthians 12:26, RSV). The counselor and a group, therefore, are concerned with the welfare of each member. Member problems that affect the group take several shapes.

Incidents Associated with Individual Members

The Absentee. In the initial exporatory interview, the counselor stresses the importance of group attendance. Group climate, structure, and function are altered with the absence of a member, and it does not go unnoticed; other members show tension and concern over repeated absences. Members ask the counselor if he knows why one of their number is away. They develop the ritual of "calling in" when they must be out of a session in order to keep each other informed. Absenteeism is low among those seriously committed to group counseling. Some persons drive 50 to 100 miles for each group meeting and give this date priority. Invited to a banquet, they do not send excuses as to why they cannot come (cf., Luke 14:15–20).

Several motives lie behind repeated absenteeism: hostility to the counselor or group, poor motivation for counseling, or an attempt to extract love and concern, or draw attention to oneself. Absence by some may reflect their own image of being worthless and therefore unnoticed—of little significance to others in the group. They simply cannot grasp the fact that their absence will make a difference.

If a person misses two consecutive meetings without giving notice, the counselor "follows up" with a telephone call. He seeks to separate valid from invalid reasons for the absence and to clarify intention of the person to remain in the group.

Two procedural devices are available to motivate the absentee. First, he is reminded that he is charged the same fee for each session missed. His place in the group cannot be filled until he formally terminates. Secondly, he is reminded that he has agreed to go through the leave-taking process before he formally terminates. This process is detailed later in the chapter. If he no longer wishes to continue counseling, he is requested to come for two final sessions.

The Silent Member. We have seen that the "onlooker" profits from "spectator therapy." We have also noted a group's understanding and tolerance for the shy person who has difficulty becoming communicative and overtly participative. Group members repeatedly invite but leave the silent one free not to respond. After two or three months, one member may engage in encounter with a non-participant. He may charge: "I feel uneasy with Norma. She has been in the group several months and I really don't know her. We have made ourselves vulnerable to her, but she never lets us know what she is thinking or feeling about us within herself. This makes me uncomfortable." This confrontation is a powerful invitation and stimulus. Usually it opens the closed door. The onlooker may venture forth only minutely, but hereafter he is under the aegis of the group to become more fully participative.

The counselor also takes note at times and calls a person's silence to the attention of the group, which adds to the invitation and desire to enfold the spectator. The programmic procedure of *going around* helps to equalize participation.

The Hostile Member. The Overtly hostile member is less of a problem than the one whose hostility is suppressed, disguised, or hidden. What is out in the open can be dealt with. This is true even when raw hostility is directed at the counselor or a member. Occasionally, a participant acts out his hostility by getting up and leaving. He may return after cooling off a few minutes or he may wait until the next meeting. Members are not seriously disturbed with this acting out; they will say, "We must give him freedom to leave as well as to return."

Several questions can be raised that bring hostility within bounds and under analysis. The counselor may ask the hostile member, "I wonder why your anger is directed against Evelyn? What in her evokes such strong feelings in you?" He may follow this up with, "I wonder if your anger is primarily directed at someone not in this group. Does Evelyn remind you of someone else?" This may direct anger at its real object, and shift the person's behavior from experiencing to analyzing. Otto Fenichel stresses the importance of maintaining the "experiencing ego" and the "analytic ego" in therapy.[1] Emoting without intellectual examination of what one experiences gives superficial and temporary therapeutic results. On the other hand, intellectualizing without experiencing is sterile. When a member's emoting gets out of bounds, the appeal to intellectual analysis aids in restoration of balance and control.

The counselor may deal with unmanageable hostile outbursts in another way; he may turn to the group and inquire, "How does this communication make you feel?" This question keeps communication on an emotional and interactional level. Later on he may call on the group for their analysis of the reason or cause of the outburst. A final alternative focuses on the recipient of the hostility. The counselor may question what the recipient is experiencing. This takes the center of the stage away from the hostile member and gives the recipient an opportunity for response. Counselor or group action in this instance gives support to the one attacked and helps him feed his feelings into the process. The assailant then has opportunity to cool off and consider how he causes others to react. Group members also come in to take sides so that the encounter spreads to involve the whole group.

The passively or covertly hostile member presents quite a different problem. The task is not in bringing hostile reactions under control

[1] *Problems of Psychoanalytic Technique.* The Psychoanalytic Quarterly, Inc., Albany, New York, 1941.

and analysis, but the loosening of controls and increasing an awareness of suppressed rage. His hostility needs to surface so he may directly experience it and communicate it. Counselor and members can
interpret times in which they experience his hostility but usually he
rejects these observations as untrue. He becomes aware of his feelings
best in group encounters in which he becomes overtly angry and
hostile. Only by directly experiencing does he become aware of, re-
claim, accept, and integrate into his self-image this rejected portion
of his self-experience.

The Depressed Member. Persons beginning counseling with a
high level of depression may require group and private counseling
until the depression lifts appreciably; then individual supportive
visits may end. In other instances, underlying depression may be
covered or controlled. The experienced counselor will be able to
detect hints of blueness or sadness in an occasional sigh of heaviness,
in lack of spontaneity, and preoccupation with inner feelings, slow-
ness in response, and so on.

Group events may uncover depression or the participant may
eventually unburden himself. Communication may be accompanied
by weeping. This particularly applies to delayed grief reactions. To
illustrate:

Mary was the burden bearer in the family. Emory, her husband,
for many years took refuge in invalidism, complaining of "all medi-
cally recorded ills." She worked to augment the family income, had
to discipline two teen-age sons, as well as providing emotional support for her ailing mate. A year previously, their 16-year-old son had
taken the family car without permission, and had gone joy-riding
with three friends. This was not typical behavior for him. An acci-
dent occurred and the son was killed. Mary made the arrangements
for the funeral, gave support and comfort to her family and relatives
and buried her own grief. In the third month of group counseling,
the leader commented that she "appeared sad tonight." (Timing is
very important here; the counselor should be sensitive enough to
judge when the person feels secure enough in the group to respond
to such a comment by "opening up.") Immediately, but in silence,
great sobs convulsed her.

The surprised group members sat quietly. As the sobbing decreased
in intensity, the counselor softly inquired, "Mary, can you tell us
what you have been experiencing?" Haltingly, she shared the story

of her son's death. Group members formed a cordon of support around her and encouraged her to go ahead each step in the sharing, when she protested, "I do not want to use up the group's time."

Usually the leader can count on members to telephone during the week following such an episode. They give support and acceptance and permit "the strong one" to be weak. These episodes are healing experiences, not only because hurt is aired but because the strong person permits others to minister to him. It is "blessed" for this parishioner to receive instead of give.

The counselor does not leave all pastoral caring of the bereaved to the group. He also calls during the week to check in, to ascertain what the member is experiencing, to allow further "working through," and to communicate that he is standing by.

The Incessant Talker. We have previously referred to the incessant talker or chronic monopolist as the one who talks to keep from revealing his problems and weaknesses. He counsels and advises other members or refuses to discuss anything but what's wrong with someone else—a mate, child, employer, or fellow worker. The reverse side of the coin is inability to talk about anything but one's own weakness, suffering, and failure. This may happen in every session or as a need periodically to have the group's exclusive attention. Often, such communication follows a well-grooved pattern. The story is well rehearsed, the telling is mechanical, without feeling, seldom showing creative inventiveness or alteration. If feelings are absent, the counselor's and the group's therapeutic object is to involve the person with hostile or other feelings that lie underneath. The first tack, however, gets the person involved with the group. He needs to "get out of" himself and take others into account, for he talks as though he is talking to himself; communication is not other-directed. Conversely, the group must be aided in overcoming its lethargy and inattentiveness and in becoming involved with the member.

A tape sequence demonstrates one enabling procedure with a member who had been in a group for six months. Letta complained about her physical aches and pains, disappointment with physicians, and mistreatment in work situations. These stories dated from two to eight years ago. Finally, the counselor asked members what they were seeing and experiencing. One interpreted Letta's feeling of being used and exploited. Letta went into more detail. The counselor inquired as to the relevance of past complaints to what she experienced now. She catalogued grievances in her immediate work situation. The counselor intervened a third time:

Counselor:	Letta has talked for 30 minutes. I am wondering what she really wants, what she is asking of and from the group.
Ellen:	"Does anyone hear me, do I really exist?" She is asking for someone to appreciate her and give her recognition.
Harvey:	Do you object to going to work? Do you feel you are a scapegoat?
Letta:	I feel they want me to do all the dirty work. The office file is the most disorganized one I know. I'm good at organizing a filing system. As soon as I do this, they will be ready to get rid of me.
Celeste:	I think Letta is feeling tired now.
Counselor:	I get the feeling that down underneath Letta is quite angry. (Harvey and Celeste concur)
Counselor:	What does the way Letta communicates do to you?
Celeste:	(Ignoring the question and to Letta) Sounds like you don't have a normal and pleasant work situation.
Letta:	(Gives further details)
Harvey:	(To Letta) Do you really want to be helped?
Letta:	(To Harvey) If anyone can tell me what to do, I'd be only too glad to do it.
Counselor:	For the first time in 45 minutes, Letta has acknowledged the presence and has spoken to another person in the group. I arose, walked to the window and stood three or four minutes . . .
Letta:	(Interrupting) I saw you.
Counselor:	And Letta continued to talk. But a moment ago she turned and addressed Harvey. It seems that before, she was talking to herself or to people outside this room.
Bridget:	People would ask her a direct question but she would not answer them. She would answer but it would not be related to the question.

Letta: Can anyone tell me what to do and how to do it?

Glen: (Speaks, but his voice is inaudible)

Counselor: Pardon?

Glen: I get very restless as she goes from one thing to another. I don't want to sit here and listen to this.

Ellen: I began to feel angry. I go along with Harvey's question, "Do you really want to be helped?" You just go on and on and on, and we don't exist. (Silence)

Letta: Well, I'm trying to let you all know something of what has happened to me. It seems to be not just one thing but all of my life seems involved.

Celeste: This is my first meeting. I have not heard you before but it seems to me you have condensed your story a lot.

Tina or Ellen: (With a tinge of irritation or sarcasm) She has talked a good deal in other meetings.

Letta: (Response inaudible on tape)

Counselor: (Drawing attention to Glen's nonverbal behavior) Glen was sitting over there squirming but all he did was squirm.

Glen: I guess I'm scared to death of feelings in this place. If I expressed the way I was feeling, it would come out all illogical and nasty. (Silence)

Counselor: You were afraid you would express yourself illogically and unpleasantly?

Harvey: (Does not allow Glen time to respond) How does one express the truth in love and yet share intuitively insight about Letta? I can sense the trap and maze you are in, Letta. You can't find a way out. You keep getting hurt and getting yourself in trouble. I can identify with the hurt you feel. But I don't hear, "It is me. How do I change me?"

Letta: Well, this is what makes me think it is me.

Harvey: I would agree with you.

Celeste: But you have to go through the first part of "kind of raging" . . . like in prayer, raging against God for the mess the world is in before you can come down and finally realize it is you.

Glen:	In a way she wasn't really raging.
Celeste:	I don't know what raging is (laughs, with giggles interspersed) but at least she may be raging about the office.
Counselor:	(To Glen) You did not think she was coming through with her feelings?
Glen:	I did not think she had one hell of a mad on.
Ellen:	I can sympathize with Letta because I understand what it is like to be angry underneath and to bottle up and hold on to it, because the world frowns on expressions of anger. What have I to gain if I blow up at the office? . . . It's not going to prove anything.
Bridget:	I sat here and wondered, "Why does this happen to Letta over and over and over in all areas?" I have been in a situation like this but I always have been able to take hold of the situation and make it move or do something about it. I wonder if I am different from Letta. A lot of it is circumstances—givenness in the situation—but I would take the bull by the horns early in the situation. At the office, if people yell at me, I yell back . . . or sit and take it and try to understand them as persons. I feel this frustration for you and I think you must be asking, "Why, why, why? Don't just support me and hear me, but why itself." And I feel this frustration for you.
Counselor:	Letta describes being mistreated, used, and unappreciated. Does she invite this?
Harvey:	I would say so. We do invite being put upon by the strong. We seek our own self-destruction.
Glen:	Letta, can you remember a time in your life when you were happy?
Letta:	(Describes "Pitching in, helping others, the way my mother taught me to do")
Counselor:	We have talked of several things, but a key one is Letta's inability to get her feelings into her communication. She talks in a detached, indirect way because she detaches her feelings. In this respect, she really is not present with us as she talks.

Celeste:	I am like Glen, not wanting to be illogical and express feelings. I have to get all the pieces of the puzzle put into place and then it is all right to talk.
Letta:	I was always taught in my home, "You don't wash your dirty linen in public." These things you talk about only within the family.
Tina:	Yes, it was this way with my family, too.
Counselor:	You were drilled not to talk outside the family about what bothered you?
Letta:	Yes.
Celeste:	It was the same way in my home.
Counselor:	(To Celeste, the new member) Could you tell us about it? (Celeste becomes the central person for the remainder of the period)

Without counselor intervention, Letta would have been as isolated after leaving the group as when she came. The above meeting did not help to involve her with her feelings; later encounters may accomplish this. She did become involved with the group and they with her. Several participants identified a communication problem in common with Letta.

The "Co-Counselor." Members have changing roles and roles may change in each meeting. These are sometimes *family* roles of father, mother, sibling, etc., or *therapeutic* roles of observer, peer, helper, or recipient of help. Occasionally, a member may be fixated in one role; he has only one way of relating. The co-counselor role may be adopted, to the person's detriment.

The co-counselor member feels his main function is to assist the counselor and give help to other group members. He may be unaware that his role signifies, "The group is for you but not for me." This member acts out of strength. Difficulties shared are difficulties of the past that have been successfully resolved. Seldom does he disclose existential anxiety threat or weakness in the immediate counseling situation. The counselor at some point calls this to the attention of the member and the group and they explore it together.

Those who have had considerable private psychotherapy and/or counseling before participation have worked through many typical problems of those beginning counseling. They are resource members and tend to fall into a helper role. They face the danger, however, of becoming trapped in a co-counselor role and fail to use the group for themselves. For example, one such member considered dropping out, saying, "I think hitherto I have been able to help others in the group and with some new members coming in perhaps I should stay. However, I feel my problems are different and perhaps I should return to individual counseling. When I get under stress, I get physical symptoms. It seems out of order to talk about these in the group." The counselor assured him that to share physical symptoms was in order and he decided to continue group counseling.

The New Member. The entrance of a new member can be a critical incident for the group as well as for the newcomer. How will veterans feel about the circle being broken? Will they reach out to recognize, accept, and include the rookie? In most instances, groups take steps to embrace him. They remember how it was with them and are able to empathize.

The counselor directs participants to interpret the group's covenant, agreements, purpose, and process for the newcomer. Each may take turns spontaneously, or the counselor may use a "going around" procedure. Infrequently, the newcomer gets a hostile reception from a member, who resents "having to share time to include you because right now I am preoccupied with my own problems." Before the session is over, the counselor sees to it that such behavior is examined and the rejected one and the group are given opportunity to respond. In a typical situation, the counselor elicits or gives the newcomer an opportunity to share identifying information, particularly if he has indicated through responses a desire for early participation.

Sexual Pairing and Group Intermarriage

Subgroups sometimes form, as we have noted, on the basis of sexual pairing. Infrequently, due to such alliances, two members may consider marriage. Several motivations underlie these bonds and may be nonsexual in character. The neurotically dominant, controlling, aggressive member may look for a submissive or compliant one. They seek a relationship determined by *neurotic complementarity* to each other. The more dominant one may be of either sex. Secondly, sexual pairing becomes a means *to overcome isolation*. George H. Bach observed that newcomers may use their sexual attractiveness as a

way to win friends and alleviate anxiety of aloneness in an established group.[2] A third motive grows out of fears of feelings of *sexual
inadequacy or inferiority*. Members may question their adequacy as
a male or female. Pairing becomes an attempt to prove or demonstrate
maleness or femaleness and gain new confidence in and a new image
of oneself by experimenting with new sexual roles. In this climate,
where there is freedom to talk and explore, the sexually inhibited
may come to a greater acceptance and appreciation for the sexual
dimension of their life and experience.

Whereas considerable conversation may focus on sex and pairing
relationships do form, a group protects itself against *acting out* sexual impulses. Group tension and anxiety rise when pairing relationships become critical. The group has a taboo against sexual acting
out; their anxiety acts as a brake and leads them to examine sexual
alliances and to interpret neurotic motivations. They also invest the
counselor as the authority person with tabooing such behavior.

Should sexual pairing result in the possibility of marriage, the
counselor leads the group in an analysis underlying motivations. He
further helps to get at the neurotic character of the complementary
relationship that may exist between the two. Divorcees or persons
with marital conflict often repeat the same pattern of "falling in love"
with a partner who has a similar character structure to that of the
divorced or estranged mate. The counselor and the group can also
interpret inherent resistance to change on the part of the pair and
their departure from the committed purpose of analysis and working
through of patterns of relationship based upon "neurotic" love.

This problem becomes more acutely critical if group members encourage or promote marriage between two individuals. In this case,
group members vicariously engage in personal sexual fantasies and
derive erotic gratification from the situation. The counselor inter-
venes and leads the group as a whole to examine the implications of
their matchmaking.

If the involved pair resists the group and counselor and insists on
marriage, the counselor has one further strategy. He reminds the
couple that major decisions, such as divorce or marriage, are not
made while in group counseling. A decision may stem from infantile
or unhealthy motives that gave birth to behavior causing the need

[2] *Principles of Intensive Psychotherapy* (New York: Ronald Press Co.,
1954), p. 410.

for counseling in the first place. Persons unwilling to abide by this therapeutic rule may be terminated and dropped from the group if their decision is deviant and resistive to group culture and purpose.

The counselor cannot rule out the possibility that the group may be a place where two people meet and where a relationship develops and leads to a meaningful and fulfilling marital union. He may encourage the couple to postpone marriage until they have completed counseling. Otherwise the counselor helps the couple and the group work through their change in role status and the effects of this change on group relations. The third alternative is to give one partner another group.

The Termination Process

The process of termination depends upon whether the group is an "open" group or one where the "end" is predetermined from its beginning. *Open groups* are those that have no terminal date; periodically, one participant leaves and is replaced by a new member. In the initial exploratory interview, no length of time is set; persons are advised that they may leave at the point when they feel they have derived maximal benefit. Decision and responsibility for "setting an end" is left to each person.

One rule prevails in the leave-taking process. A member must announce in one session his intention to leave and for several reasons, attend an additional meeting. The interval of one week provides time to reconsider a decision to terminate. Decisions may be prompted by transient episodes of anxiety, tension, despair, or anger. These feelings may spring up from *within* with no tangible external cause, or they signify fight or flight from environmental conflict in the group, family, church, or work. The week's interval allows time for a cooling off and for reconsideration.

In the second place, the group needs opportunity for response. Typically, a participant waits until the last five minutes of the hour to announce his intention, or he seeks to work this out privately with the counselor. The group is left with inadequate time or opportunity for response. Members may have "unfinished business" with the leave-taker. Either positive or negative feeling toward him may not have been previously communicated. A sudden departure can leave a group with feelings of hostility and/or guilt. Attendance at the next meeting allows also for examination of the reasons for leaving and readiness to leave. This process gets priority attention. The counselor or a member sees that ample time is reserved if the person himself does not take initiative and reopen the subject.

"Drop-outs" are those who leave before making significant therapeutic progress. Some leave for *financial reasons*, although finances often serve as an excuse for leaving. The counselor adjusts the fee rate if the person really wants to continue. Groups lose members, too, because of *geographical mobility*: a participant leaves for college or is transferred by his firm to another city.

Occasionally, *unsuitable candidates* are placed in a group with the hope or expectancy that their motivation may increase or their strong defenses yield. However, they may terminate after a short time, or the counselor may decide to terminate them and schedule a private conference to discuss this. For example, the counselor may have to terminate the incessant talker unless this member learns the art of dialogue. A person may not "fit" in one group and will require transfer to try out in another. His characteristic role may already be filled in one group, but is open and needed in a second group. Likewise, the counselor chooses a replacement for a vacated position with care in order to preserve group balance.

The termination process is different when the end of sessions for all members is predetermined from the onset. Here, all members are terminated at the same time. Each is aware of the time limit and of the approaching end. The counselor observes a gradual cessation of deep personal sharing and of dramatic interaction two or three sessions before the terminal date. Members become more silent and less participative. Near termination time, counselor exploration unearths feelings of bereavement when groups have existed for six to nine months. Members work through a sense of loss as they express appreciation to one another, comment on positive values they have experienced, and voice regret over disbanding.

Their communications may include parts of the following summation: Modern man has lost his soul—that is, his experience of identity and authentic selfhood. Uprooted and isolated, he increasingly becomes depersonalized in an impersonal society. Group counseling helps those *out of touch* with self, neighbor, and God to re-enter these three dimensions of community. In the church setting, the counseling group embodies the Beloved Community indwelt by

Christ through the Holy Spirit. In the encounter with Christ in one's neighbor and brother, we find our true life, which is hidden with Christ in God (Col. 3:3). Selfhood is called forth, discovered, and affirmed by involvement in, encounter with, and commitment to this caring community and its Lord.

BIBLIOGRAPHY

BACH, GEORGE R. *Intensive Group Psychotherapy*. New York: The Ronald Press, 1954. 446 pages. The best single volume for a comprehensive and practical description of group psychotherapy.

CARTWRIGHT, DORWIN, and ALVIN ZANDER (eds.). *Group Dynamics: Research and Theory*. Evanston: Row, Peterson & Co., Second edition, 1960. 642 pages. A choice collection of articles by action-oriented researchers which illuminate in a systematic way aspects of group formation, structure, pressures and standards, and goals and leadership.

CASTEEL, JOHN L. (ed.). *Spiritual Renewal Through Personal Groups*. New York: Association Press, 1957. 220 pages. How "small, intimate meetings of laymen can help them grow in faith and bring new life to their church."

CORSINI, RAYMOND J. *Methods of Group Psychotherapy*. New York: McGraw-Hill Book Co., Inc., 1957. 251 pages. The best single-volume review of the literature on group psychotherapy with the author's own views included.

DOUGLASS, PAUL F. *The Group Workshop Way in the Church*. New York: Association Press, 1956. 174 pages. How group work methods enable persons in the church to grow spiritually, discover their unique role and gifts, and develop leadership potentials.

DRIVER, HELEN I., et al. *Counseling and Learning Through Small-Group Discussion*. Madison, Wis.: Monona-Driver Book Co., textbook edition, 1962. 464 pages. Two works under one title: the first part is the author's discussion of multiple counseling, philosophy, and methodology; the second, a symposium to which 37 professional writers contribute.

GORDON, THOMAS. *Group-Centered Leadership*. Boston: Houghton Mifflin Co., 1956. 366 pages. An excellent demonstration of client-centered philosophy and methodology applied to the understanding of group function and leadership.

HARE, A. PAUL; EDGAR F. BORGATTA, and ROBERT F. BALES (eds.). *Small Groups: Studies in Social Interaction* New York: Alfred A. Knopf, 1955. 666 pages. Many previously unpublished research papers on behavior of small groups which will be of more interest to the advanced student of group theory.

KLAPMAN, J. W. *Group Psychotherapy: Theory and Practice*. New York: Grune & Stratton, Second revised edition, 1959. 305 pages. A didactic approach to group psychotherapy.

KLEIN, ALAN F. *Role Playing in Leadership Training and Group Problem Solving.* New York: Association Press, 1956. 176 pages. A detailed and case-illustrated guide in the use of role playing.

PARKER, WILLIAM R., and ELAINE ST. JOHNS. *Prayer Can Change Your Life.* Experiment and Techniques in Prayer Therapy. Englewood Cliffs, N.J.: Prentice-Hall, Inc., 1957. 270 pages. The authors discuss their theories and procedures of prayer therapy conducted under skilled leadership and compare their results with two other control groups.

PHILLIPS, HELEN U. *Essentials of Social Group Work Skill.* New York: Association Press, 1957. 180 pages. The author treats four areas of skills: use of limits defined by the purpose and function of the agency, use of feelings, the immediate situation, and member relationships.

POWDERMAKER, FLORENCE B., and JEROME D. FRANK (eds.). *Group Psychotherapy: Studies in Methodology of Research and Therapy.* Cambridge: Harvard University Press, 1953. 615 pages. Report of research with clinic and hospitalized patients conducted by an interdisciplinary team of 31 members under the supervision of the editors. Research was financed by the Veterans Administration and under the auspices of the Washington School of Psychiatry.

ROSENBAUM, MAX, and MILTON BERGER (eds.). *Group Psychotherapy and Group Function.* New York: Basic Books, Inc., 1963. 690 pages. Selected readings which cover areas such as history, theory, techniques, and new trends in group psychotherapy.

SLAVSON, S. R. *Analytic Group Psychotherapy.* New York: Columbia University Press, 1950. 275 pages. A companion volume to the author's earlier book, *An Introduction to Group Psychotherapy* (1943), in which he discusses a psychoanalytic group therapy approach to the treatment of children, adolescents, and adults.

SLAVSON, S. R. (ed.). *The Fields of Group Psychotherapy.* New York: International Universities Press, Inc., 1955. 338 pages. An extension of an earlier volume, *The Practice of Group Therapy* (1947), the more recent book discusses use of group therapy in various settings, such as private practice, hospitals, and industry, plus treatment of special problems—alcoholism, delinquents, sex and marriage problems, etc. Final chapters focus on training and research.

THELEN, HERBERT A. *Dynamics of Groups at Work.* Chicago: The University of Chicago Press, 1954. 379 pages. Research from the Human Dynamics Laboratory of the above university of value to the pastoral group counselor and of special interest to those concerned with the relevance of group dynamics for the classroom and social action in the community.

WITTENBERG, RUDOLPH. *So You Want to Help People: A Mental Hygiene Primer for Group Leaders.* New York: Association Press, 1947. 174 pages. *The Art of Group Discipline: A Mental Hygiene Approach to Leadership.* New York: Association Press, 1951. 124 pages. Two excellent books by the same author who makes the way plain for those new to the field of group dynamics theory.

INDEX